RAND

Changes in High School Grading Standards in Mathematics, 1982-1992

Daniel Koretz, Mark Berends

Prepared for the
College Entrance Examination Board

***RAND** Education*

The research described in this report was prepared for the College Entrance Examination Board.

ISBN: 0-8330-3073-6

Published 2001 by RAND
1700 Main Street, P.O. Box 2138, Santa Monica, CA 90407-2138
1200 South Hayes Street, Arlington, VA 22202-5050
201 North Craig Street, Suite 202, Pittsburgh, PA 15213-1516
RAND URL: http://www.rand.org/
To order RAND documents or to obtain additional information, contact Distribution Services: Telephone: (310) 451-7002; Fax: (310) 451-6915; Email: order@rand.org

Preface

In recent years, many observers have expressed concern about "grade inflation"—that is, increases in the grades given to students at any given level of achievement. Anecdotal reports suggest substantial inflation both in many high schools and in postsecondary institutions. The possibility of inflation at the high school level is a serious concern to many selective postsecondary institutions, in that it may bias their admissions decisions and may make it increasingly difficult to distinguish among high-achieving students. Grade inflation would also be troubling to many K–12 educators and policymakers. Education reform currently focuses on establishing high standards for achievement, and grade inflation could threaten that intent.

Despite the importance of grade inflation and the widespread reports of it, there has been little systematic research exploring changes in grading standards—which would include grade inflation—in U.S. high schools.

Accordingly, with support from the College Entrance Examination Board, RAND undertook an evaluation of changes in high school grading standards across the nation as a whole from 1982 to 1992. This study focused primarily on mathematics because it was possible only in mathematics to adjust grades to take into account tested achievement. This report presents the results of that evaluation.

Contents

Figures

Tables

Summary

In recent years, many observers have maintained that grades in secondary and postsecondary institutions have become inflated. Anecdotal reports of grade inflation, in some instances seemingly egregious, are common, but few studies have attempted to evaluate systematically changes in grading standards over time.

This study explores changes in high school grading standards by comparing the senior cohorts of 1982 and 1992. The data used are nationally representative surveys, the High School and Beyond study (HSB, for the 1982 cohort) and the National Education Longitudinal Study of 1988 (NELS-88, for the 1992 cohort). The study explores how the distribution of grades changed over that time, how those changes varied across types of students and schools, whether the relationship between tested achievement and grades changed between 1982 and 1992, how grades changed when changes in tested proficiency and course-taking were taken into account, and whether the predictors of grades changed over that decade. Descriptive analyses were carried out for overall high school grade point average (GPA) and for academic GPA in several subject areas. Multivariate analyses were restricted to mathematics because the surveys provided equatable tests only in that subject, making it impossible to control for changes in proficiency in the other subject areas. Efforts were made to use Scholastic Aptitude Test (SAT) and American College Test (ACT) scores as surrogates in other subjects, but that approach was abandoned after analyses showed substantial changes in the self-selection of the tested subsamples between 1982 and 1992.

The term "grade inflation" typically refers to an increase in the average grades attained by students with a given level of proficiency in the material grades are supposed to represent. This change in grading standards, however, which is called "mean shift" inflation in this report, is not the only way in which grades might become inflated. Another form of possible inflation is labeled "decreased correlation." This refers to a weakening of the relationship between proficiency and grades, such that low achievers are penalized less and high achievers rewarded less by the grading system. This report examined both of these possible changes in grading standards.

Despite the widespread discussion of grade inflation, these analyses did not show substantial grade inflation between 1982 and 1992. Indeed, they suggested that if changes in tested proficiency are taken into account, grades were deflated over the period, at least in academic mathematics courses. Simple descriptive analyses showed an increase in mean grades and in the percentage of grades above a grade of B or better, but these increases were mostly very small. For example, overall academic GPA increased by only 0.07 on a scale of 0 (F) to 4.3 (A+)—that is on a scale in which the change from a B– to a B would be 0.30. The frequency of grades of B or better increased by 3.1 percentage points. Overall changes in specific subject areas were similarly small. However, the increase was considerably larger among high-income students and in urban schools: Overall mean grades increased by 0.21 for the former group and by 0.22 in the latter.

During the same period, however, performance on the mathematics tests included in the HSB and NELS surveys, which were linked to be on the same scale, increased by about one-third of a standard deviation.[1] At the same time, the relationship between performance on the test and academic mathematics GPA *increased*. After disattenuating for unreliability (which was greater in HSB than in NELS), the correlation increased from 0.47 to 0.58. When the increase in tested proficiency was controlled, mean grades actually *declined* for all but high-scoring students. Because of the increase in the correlation between test scores and GPA from 1982 to 1992, this decrease in adjusted GPA was larger among lower-scoring students; it was 0.16 for students whose scores were at the mean and 0.35 for students whose scores were a standard deviation below the mean. Between 1982 and 1992, the number of mathematics courses taken by the average student increased markedly, as did enrollment in some courses traditionally considered college preparatory. To the extent that the data allow adjustment for these trends in course-taking, however, they appeared to have had little effect on changes in grades. Controlling for changes in both course-taking and tested proficiency again showed deflation of mathematics grades, albeit slightly less substantial than appeared when only test scores were controlled. A multivariate analysis of the prediction of academic mathematics GPA by student- and school-level variables found only modest changes from 1982 to 1992.

---

[1]Throughout this report, we maintain a distinction between "linking" and "equating" as methods of placing scores from two different tests, or two different forms of the same test, on the same scale. In modern usage, "linkage" is a more general term that refers to a range of statistical techniques that place the scores from two tests on a single scale. Linkage does not necessarily make tests functionally equivalent; for example, linked tests may contain somewhat different content, so that it is not a matter of indifference to some individuals which test they take. In contrast, "equating" refers to methods that endeavor to make tests as nearly equivalent as is practical. For example, successive forms of the SAT are equated, so it is not a matter of importance to students which form they take. The NELS and HSB tests were not constructed to be equivalent and, therefore, a linkage of the two cannot be considered an equating. The implications of this for our findings are discussed below where pertinent.

The analyses reported here have several important limitations. The test scores used to adjust for changes in proficiency were not ideal. Although the NELS and HSB mathematics tests had sufficient similarity and overlap to permit use of a conventional equating method, they were not equivalent, and differences between them may have contributed to the findings, e.g., the stronger relationship between grades and scores found in NELS. More important, the HSB and NELS tests were general-purpose survey tests and do not provide a measure of mastery of the specific content pertinent to grades in each course. Coursework variables were also limited in important ways. Courses with similar titles may vary markedly in content, for example, and the mix of content subsumed by any given course title might have changed between 1982 and 1992, perhaps as a result of the large increases in course-taking. Thus, analyses using better variables might have produced somewhat different results, but given the pattern of results reported here, it seems unlikely that they would have shown score inflation.

What accounts for the inconsistency between this study, which found no evidence of overall grade inflation between 1982 and 1992, and the widespread reports of high school grade inflation? There are at least three possibilities. One is that inflation has occurred but not during the decade examined here. A second possibility is that increases in grades in some schools, such as schools serving high-income families, may have attracted attention and may have been misconstrued as an indication of more widespread grading changes. Yet another possibility is that grading standards were not as harsh in the past as some observers believe and that examples of overly lenient grading would not be restricted to the present, if similar information were available about earlier cohorts.

Grading standards warrant further research, not only because of their importance to selective postsecondary institutions but also because of the centrality of standards to the current reform movement in K–12 education. It would be important to explore, for example, whether grades were inflated during other time periods, and the incidence and distribution of overly lenient grading would be an important issue regardless of trends over time. Further research should not be restricted to the use of large survey databases, which are a good tool for providing a first look at issues of this sort but lack the detail needed to explore them in depth.

Acknowledgments

This research project benefited greatly from the assistance of several individuals and organizations. We are grateful to the College Entrance Examination Board, which provided the funding for this work, and to Wayne Camara, the board's Vice President for Research and Development, who sponsored this work and provided thoughtful ideas and suggestions over the course of the project. We also thank Ernest Kimmel and Janice Scheuneman, who shared preliminary findings from their own analyses of grade inflation and offered comments on our work.

This report was conducted under the aegis of RAND Education. Several RAND colleagues provided support and guidance along the way. We are grateful to Thomas Sullivan, who provided the statistical support for the analyses reported here, took the lead in the linking of the NELS and HSB test scores and drafted Appendix A. Daniel McCaffrey, a statistician at RAND, provided helpful guidance and suggestions. Christel Osborn provided support in preparing the document, and we thank her for her help. The report was improved by the thoughtful suggestions of our RAND reviewers, Larry Hanser and Brian Stecher, and we would like to thank them for their timely reviews and insights.

Despite the support and guidance of these individuals and agencies, errors in this report are solely our responsibility.

1. Introduction: The Importance of Grading Standards

Although colleges and universities rely on many factors in selecting students for admission, high school grades and scores on admission tests such as the Scholastic Aptitude Test (SAT) or the American College Test (ACT) are typically the most important. Colleges rely heavily on test scores and grades because they are believed to provide important and not entirely overlapping information about students' likelihood of success in college.

Although the use of the SATs and ACTs has been the subject of intense debate in recent years, the use of high school grades as a basis for admissions is also problematic for two reasons. First, grades are affected by both subjectivity and the varying standards and purposes of teachers' grading practices (Pilcher, 1994; Brookhart, 1993; Stiggins, Frisbie, and Griswold, 1989). Admissions officers may try to address inconsistencies in grading by taking into account the characteristics and standards of individual high schools, but their ability to do so is limited, and they cannot take into account inconsistencies within schools. Second, many observers have argued that grades in both secondary and postsecondary institutions have become inflated in recent years (Turnbull, 1985; Adelman, 1982; Keith, 1982). That is, they have argued that any given level of performance receives a higher average grade now than in years past.

High school grade inflation would be a concern to postsecondary institutions for two reasons. It could erode their ability to identify promising students—for example, if grades of A encompassed a wide range of performance, or if inflation varied substantially across schools. Some observers maintain that the shift has been so substantial that grade point averages (GPAs) from some schools are no longer useful to selective postsecondary schools attempting to identify able students. In addition, some observers are concerned that overly lenient high school grades may give students unrealistic expectations concerning their ability to handle the demands of postsecondary education.

However, despite these claims, the research evidence showing grade inflation over time is scarce. Only a few studies have analyzed national data to examine whether the relationships between student grades and test scores have changed over time. Generally, these studies show that grade inflation is more prevalent in certain subjects, such as mathematics, science, and foreign languages, or for certain students—those at the higher end of the grade point distribution (Adelman, 1982; Ziomek and Svec, 1995).

In addition, *understanding* changes in grade distributions is not as simple as quantifying them. Changes in the grade distribution may stem from many factors other than trends in grading standards, such as changes in actual student proficiency, in course-taking patterns and track placement, and in the characteristics of the student population (such as an increase in the proportion of students for whom English is a second language). Moreover, changes in grading standards may have varied among important subgroups of the population, such as high- and low-achieving students, minority and nonminority students, rich and poor students, or students in urban and suburban schools. Understanding variations among important subgroups may be important for determining policy responses to changes in grading practices.

In response to these gaps in our knowledge, we conducted a series of descriptive and multivariate analyses of nationally representative data between 1982 and 1992 to understand the trends in high school grades and their correlates over the course of a decade.

Research Questions

We analyzed nationally representative data to examine trends in high school grades between 1982 and 1992, looking not only at changes in the grade distribution over time but also at concomitant changes in the educational system and in the characteristics of the student population that might have contributed to the trends or may help interpret them. In this report, we address the following research questions:

- Over the decade from 1982 to 1992, were there substantial changes in the distribution of high school grades, either overall or for certain subjects? If so, how substantial has it been and how has it varied (e.g., between males and females, minority and nonminority students, and poor and rich students)?

- Did trends in grading standards vary across types of schools?

- Did the relationship between grades and student performance on achievement tests change over time?

- How did grades change when the influence of changes in tested proficiency and course-taking is taken into account?

- What student- and school-level factors influenced grades, and did those relationships change substantially between 1982 and 1992?

Analytical Approach

We addressed these questions by analyzing nationally representative data on student background and family characteristics, school characteristics, and student course-taking during secondary school. We employed a variety of exploratory and multivariate analyses.

A comparison of High School and Beyond (HSB) to the National Education Longitudinal Study of 1988 (NELS)—both nationally representative longitudinal databases collected by the U.S. Department of Education—provides information on changes in grading and on factors that may have influenced them. These databases include information on student, family, and school characteristics; course-taking; track placement; grades; and short test batteries in different subject areas (e.g., mathematics and reading). In addition, SAT and ACT scores are available for some students. Although the HSB and NELS test batteries have important differences, they have been linked both by the Educational Testing Service (ETS) and by RAND. The linking of these test batteries is sufficiently strong to justify using the linked scores as a basis for judging changes in grading standards (see Berends, Sullivan, and Lucas, 1999). The richness of HSB and NELS makes them the best data, to date, for addressing the questions noted above.

Organization of the Report

In the next section, we briefly review the research on grade inflation at both the secondary and postsecondary levels. In Section 3, we discuss the data and methods used in the analysis. In Section 4, we present descriptive comparisons of grade distributions in 1982 and 1992 by different student and school characteristics. Section 5 focuses on the relationship between mathematics grades and both tested proficiency and course-taking patterns. In Section 6, we discuss the results from cross-sectional models that examine the variation in grading standards across different school contexts. In Section 7, we summarize the conclusions and discuss the implications of our analysis.

2. Grade Inflation: Anecdotes and Systematic Evidence

A number of editorials have appeared in the news about the alleged problem of grade inflation in America's secondary and postsecondary institutions. For example, Zirkel (1999) reported on the graduation ceremonies of two schools, each of which had 16 valedictorians who all achieved a 4.0 (straight A) average during their four years of high school. One observer wrote of a school in Pennsylvania in which an A average may just barely get a student to rank in the top 50 in his or her class because 48 of the 950 graduates received a 4.0 average for their high school career (Solomon, 1998a, 1998b).

Such anecdotes, and there are many others, have led some to conclude that grade inflation is a social and economic cancer. The term "grade inflation" is a euphemism, but the phenomenon is not the benign or insignificant statistical artifact that its name implies. Rather, grade inflation implies a kind of educational fraud, and if present, it would present hard evidence of what the *Nation At Risk* report termed "a rising tide of educational mediocrity" (National Commission on Excellence in Education, 1983, p. 5).

Despite these anecdotes, generalizable empirical evidence about grade inflation is surprisingly thin. Here, we briefly review the studies that examine grade inflation at the secondary and postsecondary levels.

Grade Inflation in Secondary Schools

The research evidence showing grade inflation over time in secondary schools is scarce. We know of only two studies that have examined changes in the distribution of grades over time for different student cohorts. Only one of these examined changes in the GPA distribution by student test scores.

One study (Adelman, 1982) analyzed student transcript data for several cohorts between 1969 and 1981. Adelman examined the discrepancy between students' self-reported grades and transcripts to gauge the inflation of self-reported grades and investigated changes in grades on transcripts between 1975 and 1981. Not surprisingly, when comparing student self-reported grades to the grade information obtained directly from the students' transcripts, Adelman found that the student self-reports were inflated in all cohorts. For example, during the

1975–1981 period, the GPA for academic track students was 2.83 in their transcripts compared to their self-reported GPA of 3.09. Examining changes over time in the transcript grades for different courses, Adelman found an increase in both high and low grades. That is, for students in college-track courses, although achievement scores declined, both the percentage of As and Bs and the percentage of Ds and Fs increased, and the percentage of Cs decreased.

Adelman summarizes his analyses across courses by stating, "Grade inflation, while significant, was not as pervasive during this time period as assumed" (p. 1). Grade inflation was more pronounced in mathematics, and to some extent science and foreign languages, as well as among students in the general track, which expanded significantly during the time period analyzed. For example, between 1975 and 1981, there was a 16.5 percent increase in the mean grades for algebra 1, a 12 percent increase in advanced mathematics, and a 16 percent increase in both Latin and general science. Yet, for a number of other course titles (e.g., sociology, literature, and health education), grades remained stable or even declined over this time period.

Ziomek and Svec (1995) found evidence of grade inflation in the cohorts graduating from 1990 to 1994 in over 5,000 public schools. They placed schools into deciles based on their mean ACT scores and then examined changes in both grades and ACT scores within each decile. They included only students who had complete ACT scores and who had taken at least three courses in at least three of the four content areas of mathematics, science, social studies, and English. Ziomek calculated the mean difference in GPAs, standardized within deciles, between graduates in their baseline year of 1990 and the graduates in each of the following four cohorts.

They found that, overall, GPAs increased from 2.94 in 1989–1990 to 3.04 in 1993–1994, whereas ACT scores remained roughly constant within each of the deciles. They also found that

- The increases in standardized grade differences were more prominent in later cohorts than in earlier ones. For example, in 1993–1994, the overall average standardized difference of GPAs across ACT deciles was 0.16 compared with the 0.03 difference in 1990–1991.

- The large increases in the standardized differences of GPAs occurred within the upper deciles of the ACT distribution (i.e., deciles 7–10). For instance, in the 10th decile, the standardized difference of GPAs was 0.21 in 1993–1994 compared with 0.06 in 1990–1991, whereas the standardized difference in the 1st decile was 0.12 in 1993–1994, even though that increased from the 0.03 difference in 1990–1991.

- Grade inflation appears to be especially significant for GPAs greater than 3.50 across all ACT decile categories. For example, the percentage of students in the 3.5–4.00 GPA range and scoring in the 10th ACT decile increased from 26 percent in 1989–1990 to 33 percent in 1993–1994. For the most part, the percentages of students with GPAs below 3.00 and scoring in the 10th ACT decile declined over the time period examined.

In short, they found evidence of grade inflation over the time period studied, particularly for students at the higher end of the grade point distribution.

Grade Inflation in Colleges and Universities

Institution-specific reports of grade inflation in postsecondary institutions abound (see Zirkel, 1999; Stone, 1995). For example, Alexander (1993) reported that in the early 1990s, 80 percent of Princeton undergraduates received nothing but As and Bs, and at Stanford only 8 percent received Cs and Ds and none received Fs, and at Williams, nearly half graduated with honors. In a nationally representative sample of nearly 5,000 undergraduates, Levine (1994) examined the proportion of students with GPAs of A– or higher and found that the figure quadrupled between the late 1960s to the early 1990s. Other studies of colleges and universities in the United States have found that GPAs of students receiving bachelor's degrees rose nearly 0.5 points between the mid-1960s and 1980s (Rogers, 1983; Kolevzon, 1981; Birnbaum, 1977).

Simple changes in the distribution of grades, without consideration of actual changes in achievement, need not indicate grade inflation, but there is some evidence that changes in postsecondary grades do at least in part reflect inflation. Stone (1995) argued that the reported rise in undergraduate GPAs was not accompanied by an increase in tested achievement as measured by the Graduate Record Exam (GRE) over this time period. The GRE is not designed as an achievement measure, so this finding is not definitive, but it is suggestive. Indeed, the simple magnitude of changes in grading described by Levine and others adds credence to the hypothesis that grades have become inflated.

The focus of our analyses is grade inflation at the high school level. In the sections that follow, we focus on nationally representative data of high school students—their GPAs, tested achievement, and other individual and school characteristics—to examine whether grade inflation exists and the factors that may explain changes in the relationship between achievement and grades.

3. Data and Methods

We analyzed nationally representative datasets that describe the experiences of high school students in the United States in the early 1980s and early 1990s. The databases are the HSB survey and NELS.

High School and Beyond

HSB is a nationally representative, longitudinal study that includes an array of information on students and schools. HSB is a two-stage stratified probability sample with schools as the first-stage units and students within schools as the second-stage units. In the first stage, 1,100 schools were selected and in the second stage, about 36 students were randomly selected in each school. Some types of schools were oversampled to ensure that adequate numbers of students were available in the subpopulations of interest. We analyzed the subset of the total sample of students who participated in the base year as sophomores and the first follow-up as seniors (see Jones et al., 1983a) and who had information from the school administrator surveys, student questionnaires, cognitive tests, and transcript files.

As part of the second follow-up, information was collected from student transcripts, including student course-taking histories and grades. Of the total HSB sample of about 26,000 students who were seniors in 1982, over 18,000 were randomly selected to constitute the target sample for the transcript study (Jones et al., 1983b). The sampling procedures were a compromise between two competing objectives: (1) the need for subgroup samples of sufficient size for complex multivariate policy analyses, and (2) the desire to avoid undue losses in statistical power because of disproportionate sampling. Of the nearly 18,000 students in the target sample, transcripts were received for 88 percent, resulting in a sample of 15,941. Of these students, about 1,000 transferred during their high school career and were deleted from our sample. Additional cases were dropped because they lacked needed information from the school administrator survey, the student survey, or cognitive testing. Thus, the final analysis sample in this report for HSB is roughly 12,400 students.

National Education Longitudinal Study

NELS is a nationally representative database that includes detailed information from students, teachers, schools, parents, and student transcript data (Ingels et al., 1995). The 1988 base-year NELS included about 25,000 eighth grade students in 1,035 schools. Some school types were oversampled to ensure that adequate numbers of students were available in subpopulations of interest. Students in NELS were followed up in the tenth grade (1990), in the twelfth grade (1992), and two years after high school (1994). A fourth follow-up was conducted in 2000. These data contain extensive information about the achievement and school experiences of students before high school entry, on school organization in middle and high school, and on students' family and demographic characteristics and on experiences beyond high school. In each of the first three waves of NELS (grades 8, 10, and 12), students were tested in mathematics, science, reading, and history.

The second follow-up of NELS also included a high school transcript study. Transcripts were obtained for over 14,000 students who participated in NELS. Because we required information from student and school administrator surveys and cognitive achievement tests, the final sample for this report was about 11,500 students.

Measures

The analyses reported here used both student-level and school-level variables. Most of the school-level variables are aggregates of student variables, but some (e.g., school locale) have no student-level counterpart or were derived from a different source. The definitions of all variables were matched across the HSB and NELS datasets; we note below where this required modifications of the original variable.

The private-school samples were not comparable in HSB and NELS. They used different sampling frames, and NELS differentiated the private sector into additional categories. Hence, we did not examine the difference between public and private schools. Private-school students were included in the file used in the descriptive analyses so that we could carry out exploratory analysis of private and public schools but were deleted from the files used in all multivariate analyses.

Student-Level Variables

GPAs. The primary focus of this study is student grades and possible changes in the distribution of grades between 1982 and 1992. Information for student GPAs was taken from the transcript files to create overall and mathematics-specific GPAs—using the conventional scale where 4.0 is an A, 3.0 is a B, 2.0 is a C, 1.0 is a D, and 0 is an F. As is conventional, in schools that used pluses and minuses, a plus added 0.3, and a minus subtracted 0.3.

All courses listed on seniors' high school transcripts were included. Almost all courses were identified in the transcript records as having been taken in grades 9 through 12. None was identified as being taken in earlier grades, but less than half of 1 percent of records lacked an indicator of the grade in which the course was taken. These records were included.

Descriptive tabulations of overall GPA excluded no courses. In specific subject areas, however, analysis was restricted to GPA in academic courses. The classification of courses as academic was based on the 1998 revision of the Secondary School Taxonomy, or SST (National Center for Education Statistics, 1999). The SST is a hierarchical classification based on a more detailed grained classification called the Classification of Secondary School Courses (CSSC), in which courses are placed into broad subject areas such as mathematics and then are broken down into progressively finer classifications. We excluded courses in categories noted as vocational, remedial, special education, and English as a second language. Our rules were as follows:

- Mathematics: exclude SST category 1_19 (vocational, etc.) and CSSC codes starting with 52, 54, or 56 (primarily special education).

- Science: include all science and engineering courses with SST codes starting with 1_2, but exclude courses with CSSC codes starting with 52, 54, or 56.

- English: include all courses with SST codes starting with 1_3 but exclude SST = 1_35 (English as a second language) and CSSC codes starting with 52, 54, or 56.

Student Achievement. The independent measure of student achievement examined here is the mathematics tests in HSB and NELS, which have been linked over time to place them on the same scale. The tests were linked using Item Response Theory (IRT) methods (Lord 1980; Hambleton 1989; see Appendix A for more details of the linking procedures used in this study). When the assumptions of IRT are met, the estimation of item parameters allows one to substitute items without changing the estimates of student proficiency. Similarly, when common items are included in different tests, these items can be used as anchors to link scores on the two tests.

The NELS and HSB mathematics tests were sufficiently similar in content and contained enough common items to permit linking, and research to date suggests that the tests contain sufficient overlap across the cohorts to allow useful comparisons of students' mathematics achievement in secondary school (see Berends, Sullivan, and Lucas, 1999; Rock et al., 1985b; Rock and Pollack, 1995).[1] However, it is important to bear in mind that although the scales of the two tests are linked to account for differences in difficulty, the tests are different enough that they cannot be considered fully equivalent even after linking. Several instances in which remaining differences between the tests may have affected our analyses are noted below. Linking of the NELS and HSB tests was not possible in other subject areas.

Race/Ethnicity. Both surveys included items to identify students' racial/ethnic group. Descriptive analyses distinguished between African Americans, Hispanics, Asians, and non-Hispanic whites. For reasons of sample size, Asians were omitted from multivariate analyses. For these analyses, we included dummy variables to indicate African American (or black) and Hispanic (or Latino); the omitted comparison group was non-Hispanic whites.

Gender. Gender was included as a dummy variable, equal to one if the student was female.

Mother's Education. Each high school senior cohort survey provided information to create a measure for mother's years of education, coded as 10 if the mother did not finish high school, 12 if the mother was a high school graduate, 14 if the mother attended some college, 16 if the mother received a four-year college degree, and 18 if the mother received a graduate or professional degree.

Family Income. Income posed a particularly challenging problem. First, the two surveys used different income intervals in the question given to students. HSB used eight response categories whereas NELS used 14, and the endpoints for

---

[1]To measure a broader range of abilities and the extent of cognitive gains between eighth and twelfth grades, NELS included various forms of the tenth and twelfth grade tests to avoid floor and ceiling effects. For example, tenth graders in the first follow-up test administration were given different forms of the test depending on how they scored in the eighth grade base year. In mathematics, there were seven forms, and in reading there were five forms, all differing in difficulty to provide better estimates of achievement throughout the proficiency distribution. (For further details on the psychometric properties of the NELS tests, see Rock and Pollack, 1995). It was possible to link across all these NELS mathematics forms and the NELS and HSB cohorts.

many of the eight intervals used in HSB did not correspond to those used in NELS. In addition, when incomes are changing nonuniformly, it is not apparent how income categories should be adjusted to make categories comparable over time. For example, depending on assumptions about how income differences affect performance, one might want to keep income categories fixed in terms of purchasing power, in terms of the percentages of household in each, or in terms of their relationship to some critical level of income.

We first rescaled the HSB income categories to 1992 dollars by multiplying the endpoints of each interval by the change in the Consumer Price Index (CPI) from 1982 to 1992. We then collapsed the eight income categories into five to make the endpoints of the categories more similar to the endpoints of NELS categories. The raw and adjusted income values and the categories into which we placed each of the original ranges are shown in Table 3.1. We then collapsed the 14 NELS income categories into five by aligning the endpoints of the intervals as closely as possible to the inflated endpoints of the collapsed HSB categories. This is shown in Table 3.2.

In practice, this five-level income categorization turned out not to be useful in some analyses, and it was not comparable to some earlier work that considered the relationship between low income and grades (U.S. Department of Education, 1994). Therefore, although we used all five categories in descriptive analyses, we collapsed them further into two categories for multivariate analyses. The low-income category of the dichotomous variable included the lowest two of the five income categories in Table 3.2 and had a cutoff roughly equal to 140 percent of the poverty index for a family of four in 1992.

High School Program. The HSB and NELS dataset included a question measuring the students' perceptions of their secondary school track as academic, general, or vocational. These measures provide only limited information about

Table 3.1

Raw and Adjusted Income Ranges and RAND Categories, HSB

			CPI-Adjusted to 1992 Dollars			
Low	Midpoint	High	Low	Midpoint	High	Category
—	4,000	7,999	—	5,815	11,630	1
8,000	11,500	14,999	11,631	16,719	21,807	2
15,000	17,500	19,999	21,808	25,442	29,076	3
20,000	22,500	24,999	29,078	32,712	36,346	3
25,000	27,500	29,999	36,347	39,981	43,615	4
30,000	35,000	39,999	43,617	50,885	58,154	4
40,000	45,000	49,999	58,155	65,424	72,693	4
50,000			72,694	—	—	5

Table 3.2

**Raw Income Ranges and RAND
Categories, NELS**

Low	Midpoint	High	Category
—	500	999	1
1,000	2,000	2,999	1
3,000	4,000	4,999	1
5,000	6,250	7,499	1
7,500	8,750	9,999	1
10,000	12,500	14,999	2
15,000	17,500	19,999	2
20,000	22,500	24,999	3
25,000	30,000	34,999	3
35,000	42,500	49,999	4
50,000	62,500	74,999	4
75,000	87,500	99,999	5
100,000	150,000	199,999	5
200,000			5

students' high school experience, but it is the case that this "track" variable provides useful information about students' programs and their placement within the school (Lucas, 1999; Gamoran and Berends, 1987; Gamoran, 1989). The academic group includes students who typically take courses for college-bound students (either an officially mandated program of courses or an unofficial sequence within the curriculum). Because we were interested in grading standards as they pertain to college admissions, we created a dummy variable for the academic track. The omitted group was all other students; we did not distinguish between students in the vocational track and the general track.

Course-Taking. Because we were concerned with the possible effects of changes in course-taking on the distribution of academic grades, we needed to measure the specific types of mathematics courses taken. For multivariate analyses, mathematics courses were classified using the 1998 revision of the SST (National Center for Education Statistics, 1999). Mathematics is broken into nine broad categories:

1. General mathematics,

2. Consumer mathematics,

3. Pre-algebra,

4. Algebra 1,

5. Geometry,

6. Algebra 2 through pre-calculus,

7. Advanced mathematics,

8. Unified mathematics, and

9. Occupationally related mathematics.

We considered categories 3 though 7 to be academic courses and created variables to distinguish among them. Of these, only one was subdivided in the SST: advanced mathematics was subdivided into calculus, advanced placement and international baccalaureate, and other. The content of many "unified mathematics" courses appears to be academic; the description of the revised SST notes that "Unified Mathematics was created to hold the unified coursework, previously distributed among the Algebra 1, Geometry, and Advanced Mathematics—Algebra subcategories" (National Center for Education Statistics, 1999, p. 29). However, it was not possible to determine the intended content coverage of these courses or whether that intended content was similar in 1982 and 1992. Moreover, these courses were relatively uncommon, particularly in HSB. Accordingly, these courses were included in our academic mathematics GPA measure, but we did not create an additional variable indicating coursework of this type.

Exploratory analysis indicated that it was reasonable to use only the first level of the SST classification in mathematics.

For disentangling changes in coursework from changes in grading standards, the most important consideration is the mix of coursework across types that might have different standards. Accordingly, we created variables indicating the proportion of each student's academic mathematics marks coming from courses of four types: algebra 1, algebra 2 (as defined above), geometry, and advanced. The proportion of marks from all other academic mathematics courses was necessarily omitted, as it is a linear function of the four specified proportions.

School-Level Variables

Mean Achievement. The test scores of the students in each school were aggregated to obtain a school-level achievement measure.

School Racial/Ethnic Composition. School administrators in HSB and NELS were asked about the proportion of various population groups who attended the school. Using this information, we were able to create two school-level variables that measured the proportions of African American and Hispanic students who attended each school. The alternative would have been to create these measures by aggregating information from our samples. Both approaches have drawbacks; aggregating student-level data from our reduced samples might have misrepresented the composition of some schools, whereas relying on data from administrators makes the level 1 (student) and level 2 (school) variables in our multilevel models not precisely comparable.

School Mother's Education. The student-level measure of mother's educational attainment was aggregated to the school level by taking the mean.

School Income. The school-level income variable was the proportion of students in the low-income category of the income dichotomy described above.

School Locale. Schools were either urban, rural, or suburban.[2] We created dummy variables for each with suburban as the reference (omitted) category.

School Course-Taking. The school course-taking variables were the means of the four proportions noted above. For example, one of the student-level variables was the proportion of a student's academic mathematics marks stemming from courses in algebra 1. The school mean of that variable is the average proportion of academic mathematics marks from courses in that category across sampled students.

Methods

Sample Weighting

Because students were sampled for both HSB and NELS with varying probabilities, it was necessary to weight the data to obtain comparable, representative results. Both surveys offer a variety of sampling weights representing the wave of the survey and the instrument from which variables are derived. For example, the data include base-year test weights for use with

---

[2]Locale is a seven-digit code on the Common Core of Data (CCD) of the U.S. Department of Education, defined as: 1. large city—a central city of a consolidated metropolitan statistical area (CMSA) or metropolitan statistical area (MSA), with the city having a population ≥ 250,000; 2. midsize city—a central city of a CMSA or MSA, with the city having a population < 250,000; 3. urban fringe of a large city—any incorporated place, Census-designated place, or nonplace territory within a CMSA or MSA of a large city and defined as urban by the Census Bureau; 4. urban fringe of a midsize city—any incorporated place, Census-designated place, or nonplace territory within a CMSA or MSA of a midsize city and defined as urban by the Census Bureau; 5. large town—an incorporated place or Census-designated place with a population ≥ 25,000 and located outside a CMSA or MSA; 6. small town—an incorporated place or Census-designated place with a population < 25,000 and ≥ 2,500 and located outside a CMSA or MSA; 7. rural—any incorporated place, Census-designated place, or nonplace territory designated as rural by the Census Bureau. The usual practice is to combine these into three categories: urban = 1, 2; suburban/large town = 3, 4, 5; and rural/small town = 6, 7.

students who were administered the base-year tests, as well as base-year questionnaire weights for students administered the base-year questionnaire. Because some students were administered the base-year questionnaire but not the base-year test, these weights are not identical. The weights vary more substantially across waves because of attrition. In addition, the sample for whom transcripts were obtained was substantially different from that for whom questionnaire data were obtained.

No weights were provided for the specific subsample we used (students with valid data from the questionnaire, the tests, and transcripts), and the database does not include the level of detail that would have allowed us to create those weights. Accordingly, we conducted a series of detailed analyses to determine how adequate one of the existing weights would be for our purposes. These analyses are summarized in Appendix B. We concluded that the existing transcript weights were adequate for our purposes, and all weighted analyses reported here use those weights. These weights were restandardized so that the sum of the weights was equal to 10 times the number of observations, for reasons described in Appendix B.

Descriptive Analyses

The first stage in our analysis was a series of descriptive analyses to explore changes between 1982 and 1992 in the distribution of grades, both overall and for specific groups of students and schools. These descriptive analyses are not a test for grade inflation because these they do not hold constant academic achievement (proxied later by test scores) or changes in course-taking. However, understanding the extent and location of changes in the grade distribution may help explain common perceptions of grading changes and provide a useful context for evaluating changes in grading standards.

These descriptive analyses were carried out both for total academic GPA and for mathematics grades. We compared histograms of the entire grade distributions and explored four summary measures (means, medians, and percentages above B and B+). We do not present all of the measures but comment when they provided substantially different views. Student and family characteristics used in the descriptive analysis included race/ethnicity, gender, mother's education, track, and several income variables, including both a poverty dichotomy and a categorical income variable, as described above. The only school variable used in descriptive analyses was locality (urban, rural, suburban).

Multivariate Analyses

To infer changes in grading standards from changes in the simple distributions in grades, however, it is necessary to take into account two concurrent changes: trends in the measured proficiency of students and changes in the courses they took. During the period in question, there were some changes in the measured achievement of students, particularly certain groups of students (Berends, Sullivan, and Lucas, 1999; Campbell, Hombo, and Mazzeo, 2000; Koretz, 1992). An increase in grades accompanied by an increase in measured achievement might not signify inflation. In addition, one key reform in many states during the 1980s was an increase in graduation requirements for students (Murphy, 1991). Thus, changes in grades may be a reflection of the changes between the early 1980s and 1990s in the mix of courses that students took during their high school careers.

Neither of these concurrent trends can be fully addressed analytically. To estimate changes in grading standards, one ideally would want to control for measures of achievement in the specific domains taught in each of the relevant courses, and none of the assessments available to us were that detailed. Controlling for changes in the courses taken is complicated by numerous factors. For example, courses with the same name—say, algebra 1—may be very different in content and difficulty, and one cannot assume that the mix of content and difficulty across algebra 1 courses would stay constant if the proportion of students enrolling in these classes increased substantially.

Nonetheless, steps can be taken to help disentangle these concurrent trends from changes in grading. In mathematics, but not in other subjects, we could link the mathematics tests administered in HSB and NELS and use the linked scores to control for changes in overall proficiency in commonly taught aspects of mathematics. We explored this approach using ACT and SAT scores to control for proficiency in other areas. However, we found indications of substantial and changing selectivity in the subsamples of HSB and NELS that had scores from these tests and concluded that it was not feasible to use them in a comparable manner to control for proficiency differences (see Appendix C).

Examining the possible effects of changes in course-taking was more complex. We again focused on mathematics and began by examining changes in enrollment patterns and in the grade distributions in broad categories of courses (e.g., algebra 1 and geometry). We then explored whether differences in grades among groups of courses reflected characteristics of the classes or the proficiency of students. We created coursework indicator variables for inclusion in multivariate models predicting mathematics GPA. The analyses of proficiency and coursework changes and their effects are presented in Chapter 5.

To explore the influence that other student and school characteristics may have on grades, we estimated a series of multilevel models. In these models, mathematics grades in 1982 and 1992 are a function of student characteristics (e.g., gender, race/ethnicity, socioeconomic status, and course-taking patterns) and school characteristics (e.g., locale, school income, and school racial/ethnic composition). The results of these analyses are reported in Section 6.

The NELS and HSB data are clustered because of the multistage sampling design. This clustering does not affect parameter estimates but it does bias variance estimates. The multilevel models used in the analyses reported in Chapters 5 and 6 take into account clustering of observations within schools (see Appendix D). No further adjustments for clustering were made.

4. Shifting Grades over a Decade? A Descriptive Analysis

In this section, we provide descriptive information on changes in the distribution of academic grades, overall and for important groups of students and schools. These changes do not constitute evidence of grade inflation (or of other changes in grading standards) because they do not take either course-taking or student proficiency into account. However, they do help explore common perceptions of grading changes and provide a context for investigating inflation. Following a description of total academic GPA, we provide less-detailed information about GPA changes by subject.

Total Academic GPA

Despite the widespread perception of grade inflation, the overall distribution of academic grades showed only modest changes between 1982 and 1992, with slight decreases in the frequency of grades at most levels equal to or lower than C+ and slight increases at higher levels. The percentage of students with GPAs of C+ or lower declined, whereas the percentages receiving GPAs of B– through A increased (Figure 4.1). The mean GPA increased only from 2.56 to 2.63. The

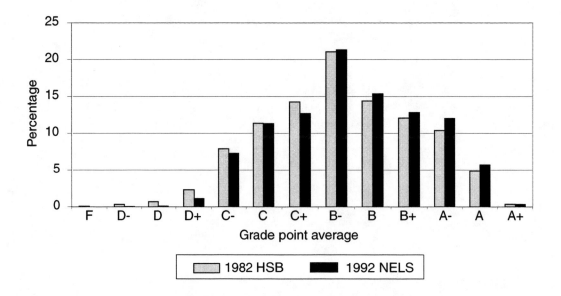

Figure 4.1—Overall Distributions of Academic GPA, 1982 HSB and 1992 NELS

percentage of students receiving a GPA of 3.0 or higher increased from 42.0 to 46.2, and the percentage of students with a GPA of 3.3 or higher increased from 27.7 to 30.8.

These small increases in GPA varied little among racial/ethnic groups. Only Hispanics showed a substantially different change in GPA from the others. Hispanics showed a substantially larger increase in mean GPA than the other groups and a slightly greater increase in the percentage of GPAs of 3.0 or more (Table 4.1). The Asian samples showed substantial but partially offsetting changes: a decrease in grades of B but an increase in B– and B+. The very small sample of Asians in HSB, as well as the substantial changes in the Asian population caused by immigration, make these patterns questionable.

Changes in grading showed no substantial differences between males and females. There were some slight differences—for example, the decrease in GPAs of C+ was slightly larger among males—but both genders experienced a small decrease in the frequency of all GPAs below a B– and a small increase in all higher GPAs.

GPAs increased slightly more for students with well-educated mothers. The academic GPAs of students whose mothers had a high school education or less showed almost no change, whereas the GPAs of those whose mothers had some college or more education increased by a larger but still small amount (Table 4.2). The greater increase in GPA among higher-educated families occurred despite the fact that this group became less selective. Students with mothers with at least some college education increased from 29 to 35 percent of the sample from 1982 to 1992, and those whose mothers had at least a college degree increased from 15 to 26 percent of the sample.[1] The small mean increase in the academic GPA of

Table 4.1

Change in Academic GPA by Race/Ethnicity, 1982 to 1992

	Mean Grade	Percentage with B or Greater
All	0.074	3.1
Asian	0.037	3.0
African American	0.050	1.8
Hispanic	0.170	4.9
White	0.056	2.5

[1]The changing distribution of mother's education accounts for the fact that the increase in GPA among all students is close to the highest value for any of the subgroups in Table 4.2.

Table 4.2

**Change in Academic GPA by Mother's
Education, 1982 to 1992**

All	0.074
Less than high school	−0.020
High school graduate	−0.004
Some college	0.081
College degree or more	0.073

students whose mothers had at least a college degree stemmed largely from a sizable increase in GPAs of A– and A (Figure 4.2).

Self-reported track had a slight relationship to the increase in mean GPA. The mean GPA of students' reporting themselves in the academic track was essentially constant, increasing only 0.01, whereas the GPA of other students increased by about 0.04.

More substantial differences in grading changes appeared across income categories. The four lower income categories all showed small changes in average GPA. Categories 1, 3, and 4 showed increases similar to the overall increase, but category 2 actually showed a small decrease in mean grades (Table 4.3). In contrast, the mean increase in the highest income category, although still smaller than a fractional grade point (e.g., from B– to B), was nearly three times as large as the overall mean increase. This mean increase reflected sizable

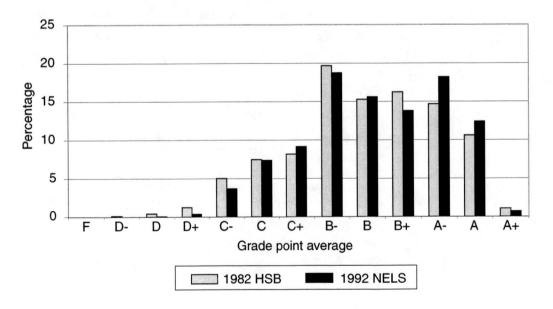

Figure 4.2—Distributions of Academic GPA Among Students Whose Mothers Have
at Least a College Degree, 1982 HSB and 1992 NELS

Table 4.3

**Change in Academic GPA by Income
Category, 1982 to 1992**

	Mean Grade	Percentage with B or Greater
All	0.074	3.1
1	0.062	1.7
2	–0.061	–3.9
3	0.077	0.1
4	0.055	1.3
5	0.211	13.0

increases in the percentages of students receiving GPAs of B+, A–, or A (Figure 4.3). In all income categories other than the highest, the change in the percentage of GPAs of 3.0 or greater was modest, whereas in the highest income category, the increase was 13 percentage points (Table 4.3), from 48 to 61 percent of all students in the category. This increase occurred even though the top income category became less selective during the decade, increasing from 10.5 percent to 14.4 percent of the weighted sample.

The change in academic GPA from 1982 to 1992 varied substantially depending on the location of schools. The mean academic GPAs of students in rural and

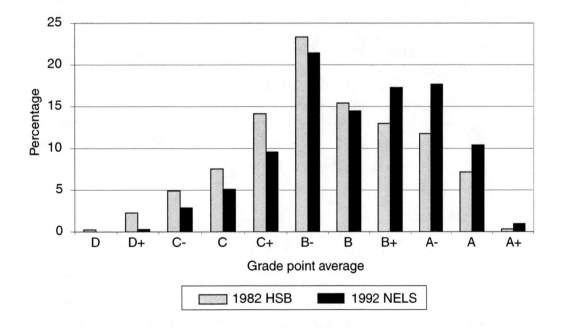

**Figure 4.3—Distributions of Academic GPA in Highest Income Category,
1982 HSB and 1992 NELS**

suburban schools increased by only about 0.04, whereas the mean GPA of students in urban schools increased by 0.22 (Table 4.4). This mean change reflects a sizable increase in the percentages of students with GPAs of B, B+, or A–.

Although simple changes in mean GPA do not necessarily correspond to grade inflation, these variations across types of students and schools might help explain the seeming inconsistency between the small aggregate change in mean academic GPA between 1982 and 1992 and the widespread perception of serious grade inflation. That is, some observers may have been more swayed by groups that had atypically large changes in GPA, such as students from urban schools or from high-income families.

Table 4.4

**Change in Academic GPA by School Location,
1982 HSB to 1992 NELS**

	Mean Grade	Percentage with B or Greater
All	0.074	0.031
Rural	0.043	0.010
Suburban	0.035	0.010
Urban	0.221	0.110

GPA Changes by Subject

Overall trends in grades could mask substantially different trends across subject areas. Because some of our analyses were necessarily restricted to mathematics—the only subject in which we had linked test scores for HSB and NELS—it was particularly important to examine simple changes in mathematics grades. We also explored trends in English and science grades.

Mathematics

Changes in academic mathematics GPA were in broad stroke similar to those for total academic GPA, although they did differ in some details.

The overall increase in mathematics GPA was even smaller than the increase in total academic GPA, but the change was inconsistent across the range of grades (Figure 4.4). Mean mathematics GPA remained roughly a C+ and increased only by about 0.04 from 1982 to 1992. Both males and females showed only a small gain in mathematics GPA, but that for males was slightly larger: 0.07 for males

23

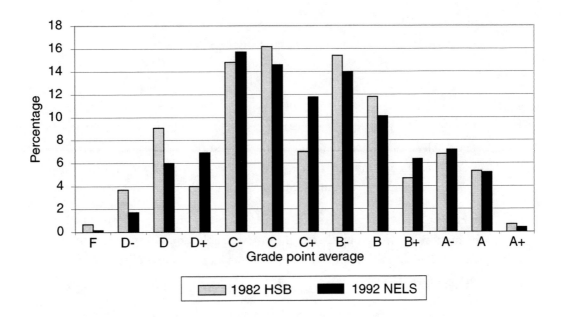

Figure 4.4—Distributions of Academic Mathematics GPA, 1982 HSB and 1992 NELS

and 0.04 for females. The change in mean mathematics GPA varied only modestly among racial/ethnic groups, ranging from a decline of 0.03 among Asians to an increase of 0.1 among Hispanics. The modest differences in grading changes across levels of mother's education appeared with mathematics GPA as well.

The sizable variation in academic GPA trends among income groups was echoed in mathematics GPA. Indeed, the differences were slightly larger in the case of mathematics (Table 4.5). The two lowest income categories showed decreases in mathematics GPA (–0.03 and –0.14, respectively), whereas the highest income category showed an increase of 0.26. The large differences in total GPA change among locales, however, was greatly attenuated in the case of mathematics GPA.

Table 4.5

**Change in Academic Mathematics
GPA by Income Category**

	Mean Grade
All	0.041
1	–0.032
2	–0.135
3	0.064
4	0.050
5	0.262

24

Rural and suburban schools showed essentially no change in mathematics GPA, and urban schools showed an average increase of only 0.06.

English

Overall, grades in academic English courses also increased only slightly, albeit a very small amount more than mathematics grades. The mean grade increased by about 0.06. As one can see from Figure 4.5, this very small increase stemmed from increases in the percentages of grades in the C+ through A– range.

In English, as in mathematics, the increase in mean grades was much larger in the highest income group than in the others (Table 4.6). The increase in grades was small in all racial/ethnic groups but was larger among Hispanics than among others (Table 4.7).

Science

The distribution of academic science grades differed substantially between HSB and NELS (Figure 4.6), but the net effect of these changes was very small. The mean grade increased by only 0.04. In science, as in other subjects, the increase in grades was substantially larger in the top income category than in others. It was also somewhat larger among Hispanics and Asians than among other students (Table 4.8).

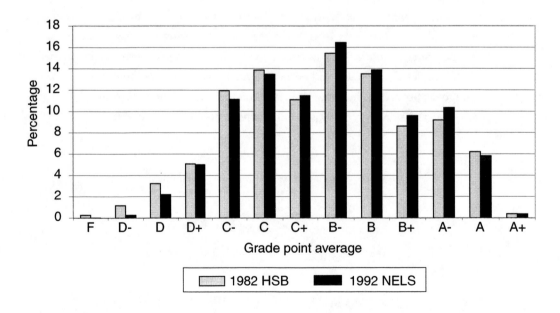

Figure 4.5—Distributions of Academic English GPA, 1982 HSB and 1992 NELS

Table 4.6

**Change in Academic English
GPA by Income Category**

	Mean Grade
All	0.063
1	0.068
2	−0.097
3	0.052
4	0.043
5	0.224

Table 4.7

**Change in Academic English
GPA by Race/Ethnicity**

	Mean Grade
All	0.063
Asian	0.069
African American	0.035
Hispanic	0.147
White	0.041

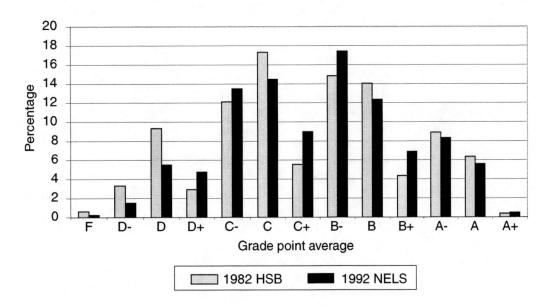

Figure 4.6—Distributions of Academic Science GPA, 1982 HSB and 1992 NELS

26

Table 4.8

**Change in Academic Science
GPA by Race/Ethnicity**

	Mean Grade
All	0.039
Asian	0.112
African American	0.017
Hispanic	0.180
White	0.007

5. Have Grades Become Inflated? Mathematics Grades in the Context of Tested Proficiency and Coursework

Although the tabulations described above portray changes in grading, they do not show changes in grading *standards*. To examine trends in grading standards, it is necessary to take into account both changes in the coursework students took and changes in their proficiency. NELS and HSB do not include enough information to control fully for changes in proficiency and coursework, but they do permit an estimate of these effects in mathematics. This section describes our estimates of changes in mathematics grades, adjusting for trends in coursework and tested proficiency in mathematics.

The section begins by describing two distinct analytical questions that are subsumed under "grade inflation" or, more generally, changes in grading standards. This is followed by descriptions of changes in tested proficiency and course-taking and of the relationships between grades and level of courses. The final subsections present estimated changes in grades with no controls, with controls for changes in tested proficiency, and with controls for changes in both tested proficiency and course-taking.

The results of these analyses suggest that in mathematics, grades were modestly *deflated* between 1982 and 1992. The small increases in raw grades described in the previous section were more than offset by increases in tested proficiency.

Two Notions of Changing Standards

Changes in grading standards could be of two types. Commonly, the term "grade inflation" is used to refer to an increase in mean grades for students with a given level of proficiency in the graded material. The notion is that a given grade signals less of value—less achievement—than it did previously. This notion implies only a shift upward in grades over time but not a change in the relationship between proficiency and grades with cohorts (e.g., Figure 5.1). We call this "mean shift" score inflation.

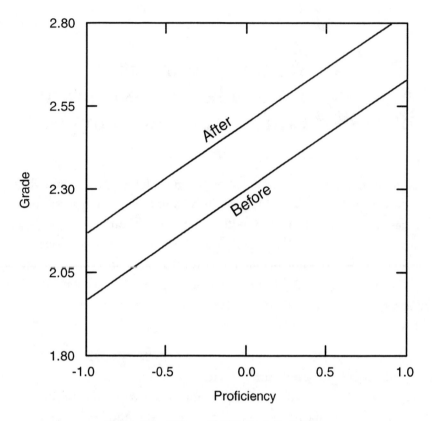

Figure 5.1—"Mean Shift" Grade Inflation

"Changing standards" might also refer to changes in the relationship between proficiency and grades within cohorts. That is, over time, grading may become either more or less strongly related to differences in actual student proficiency. In this case, grade inflation would entail a decrease in the relationship between proficiency and grades, such that grading gave less sanction to weak performers and less reward to high performers. This type of inflation, which we call "decreased correlation" inflation, entails a change in the slope of the regression of grades on proficiency (e.g., Figure 5.2).

In practice, changes in grading standards could entail both mean shifts and changes in correlation. After describing changes in proficiency, changes in coursework, and the relationships between coursework and grades, we analyze both mean shifts and changing correlations in grading standards.

Changes in Tested Proficiency

It is well known that tested proficiency in mathematics has gradually improved in recent decades. On the NAEP long-term trend assessment, the mean increase

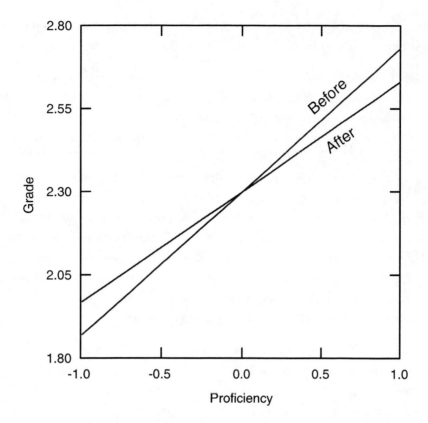

Figure 5.2—"Decreased Correlation" Grade Inflation

in mathematics during the 10 years between HSB and NELS was modest, and it occurred primarily between 1990 and 1992 (Campbell, Hombo, and Mazzeo, 2000). In the sample used in this analysis, the mean increase in linked mathematics scores between HSB and NELS was about 0.34 standard deviation. Thus, to the extent that the HSB and NELS tests measure the same skills that should be tapped in assigning student grades, one would expect that if grading standards and all else had stayed constant, mean mathematics grades would have increased by a commensurate amount—much more than the very small increases in grades described above. However, the content of these tests does not fully overlap with the content of high school courses. Thus, controlling for these test scores does not fully control for relevant aspects of proficiency in mathematics—an important limitation that is discussed further below.

Course-Taking and Its Relationships to Grades

Although students aiming for admission to selective colleges have typically taken primarily college-track courses throughout their careers, many other students have not. Over the past two decades, there has been strong pressure to increase the number of academic-track courses taken by all students, and many states have stiffened their course-taking requirements for high school graduation.

Changes in course-taking, such as an increase in participation in college-track courses, could change the distribution of grades in many ways and could distort inferences about trends in grading standards. If grading standards differ among types of classes, a change in the mix of mathematics courses taken could alter mathematics GPA even if actual performance did not change. A change in the selectivity of students taking courses—for example, an influx into advanced courses of lower-performing students whose counterparts in earlier cohorts would not have taken them—could lead teachers to change grading standards within courses. Both changes in the mix of courses taken by students and an overall increase in the number of mathematics courses taken could contribute to such a change in selectivity. Changes such as these would alter the relationship between performance and grades, making it more difficult to ascertain from simple changes in GPA whether grading standards changed.

The NELS and HSB data do not permit a thorough investigation of these questions, but we were able to explore them in several ways for mathematics. We examined changes in course-taking from 1982 to 1992 and investigated differences in grading standards between the courses that saw large increases and other courses.

Changes in Mathematics Course-Taking from 1982 to 1992

Consistent with the reform efforts of the 1980s, the decade saw a sharp increase in the number of mathematics courses taken by the average student. In 1982, the average number of mathematics courses completed per student in our sample was 3.2. Ten years later, that number had increased by more than 80 percent, to more than 5.8 courses. At the same time, there was a modest increase in participation in courses from the traditional college-bound track, such as geometry and algebra 2. The proportion of grades from general courses decreased, whereas the proportion from geometry and especially algebra 2 increased (Figure 5.3).

The modest change in the proportion of courses from each area, however, does not take into account the large increase in mathematics course-taking over the same period. The combined effect of the increase in mathematics course-taking and the shift into college-track classes is shown by trends in the number of course grades per student. The number of general course grades per student dropped slightly, while the number of grades in all categories of courses at the level of algebra 1 or higher increased (Figure 5.4). The increases were particularly large

31

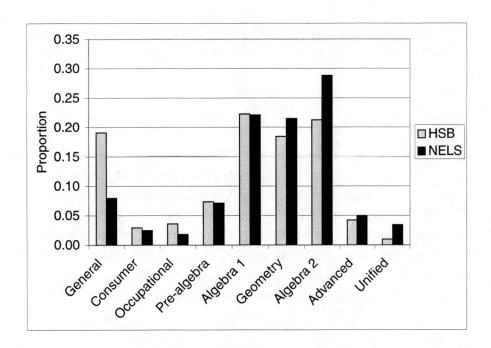

**Figure 5.3—Proportion of Mathematics Courses in Nine Categories,
1982 HSB and 1992 NELS**

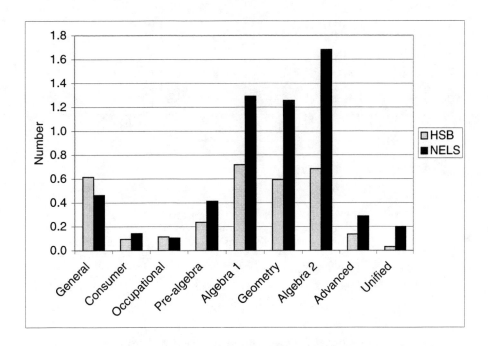

**Figure 5.4—Number of Mathematics Course Grades per Student
in Nine Categories, 1982 HSB and 1992 NELS**

in algebra 1 (80 percent), geometry (112 percent), algebra 2 (146 percent), and advanced (114 percent). Recall that unified mathematics may include content from any of the other categories.

Changes in Grades in Specific Mathematics Courses

The small changes in mathematics grades described above occurred primarily in high-level classes: geometry, algebra 2, advanced, and unified. The change was most marked in advanced classes, in which the share of students receiving a grade of 3.0 or higher increased by 10 percent, and the share receiving a grade of A– or higher increased by more than 7 percent (Figure 5.5). Of the courses that showed very large increases in participation, only algebra 1 showed no consistent increase in the percentage of high grades. Pre-algebra, which had a smaller increase in participation, showed a small decrease in grades.

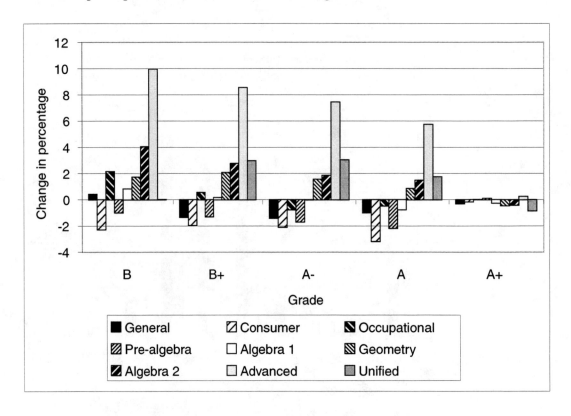

Figure 5.5—Change in Percentage of Grades at or Above Each Level
by Type of Course, 1982 HSB and 1992 NELS

The Relationships Between Course Level and Grades

The shift into higher-level mathematics courses, in conjunction with the large increase in mathematics coursework, could affect the grade distribution in several ways and could distort inferences about changes in grading standards. For example, if grading standards and the level of difficulty of courses were maintained, the movement of students into more difficult courses might be expected to depress mean grades. If grading standard were maintained but were harsher in the more advanced courses, this trend would be exacerbated. If, on the other hand, grading standards were more lenient in more advanced courses—for example, if teachers believed that an advanced class with the highest-achieving students should have a high mean grade despite the difficulty of the material—any downward trend in grades caused by the movement of students into more advanced courses would be attenuated or perhaps even reversed. And, of course, grading standards may have changed within levels of coursework, either because of a secular trend in grading standards or as a reaction to the influx of lower-achieving students into difficult courses.

In both cohorts, grades were on average higher in more advanced mathematics courses, underscoring the potential confounding between changes in coursework and grades. In both cohorts, the distribution of course grades was nearly identical across the four lowest course categories, through algebra 1 (Figure 5.6). However, geometry, algebra 2-precalculus, and advanced (which included non-AP calculus, AP mathematics courses, and other advanced courses) had progressively higher distributions of grades in both cohorts. These distributions count each course grade as an observation, and the middle line of each bar represents the median across all grades. A similar if less striking pattern appears in the average grades of individual students. Table 5.1 shows four mathematics grade point averages: the total GPA across all academic courses, the average across all algebra 1 grades, the average of algebra 2 grades, and the average across all advanced courses. In both cohorts, the mean of the advanced grades is considerably higher than the other averages. In HSB, the mean for algebra 2 was slightly higher than those for lower-level courses, although this difference had nearly vanished in NELS.

These simple comparisons, however, confound two things: differences in grading across courses and differences in the subsamples of students who contributed grades for each class. For example, in NELS, the number of students

34

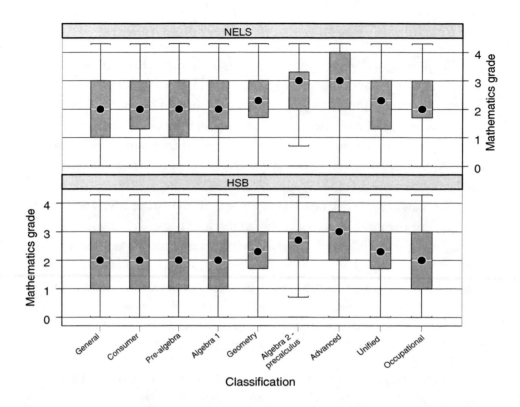

Figure 5.6—Distribution of Math Course Grades by SST Course Classification

contributing algebra 1 grades was nearly four times as large as the presumably much more selective group with grades from advanced courses. To disentangle these two factors, we created two subgroups that were homogeneous in terms of course-taking and explored differences in mean grades across courses within each of these groups. Within each of these subgroups, comparisons across courses were stripped of differences in selectivity that confound simple comparisons across courses. The larger group contained all students who had valid grades for both algebra 1 and algebra 2 but no grade for an advanced mathematics course. The second and much smaller group included students who had grades for algebra 1, algebra 2, and at least one advanced mathematics course.

When comparisons across courses are restricted in this way to consistent subgroups of students, the tendency for grades to be higher in more advanced courses is reversed. Within each of these subgroups, there was a clear tendency for grades in more advanced courses to be lower than the grades in lower-level

Table 5.1

Mean Math GPAs, Overall and for Advanced Courses

	N^a	Mean
1982 HSB		
Total academic GPA	12,324	2.20
Algebra 1 GPA	7,906	2.24
Algebra 2 GPA	5,596	2.38
Advanced math GPA	1,332	2.70
1992 NELS		
Total academic GPA	11,522	2.23
Algebra 1 GPA	8,104	2.21
Algebra 2 GPA	7,765	2.28
Advanced math GPA	2,113	2.70

[a] The number of students contributing grades to each mean.

classes (Tables 5.2 and 5.3). This seems reasonable, given the more difficult material in advanced classes, and does not suggest any confounding tendency toward more lenient grading in more advanced classes.

These consistent subgroups did show a clear change in grades, however, that is not an indication of inflation. In both cases, average mathematics GPAs for these groups dropped between 1982 and 1992. In the case of students who took algebra but not advanced mathematics, mean GPA dropped about 0.2 overall and by a similar amount in algebra 1 and algebra 2 (Table 5.2). The decrease in grades was larger for the much smaller subsample of students who took advanced courses; algebra 2 grades for these students dropped by nearly 0.4 (Table 5.3). These decreases could reflect a decline in the selectivity of upper-level courses accompanying the sizable increase in the proportion of students taking these courses.

Table 5.2

Mean Math GPAs of Students Who Took Algebra but Not Advanced Math

	N	Mean	Difference, NEL–HSB
1982 HSB			
Total academic GPA	3,704	2.47	
Algebra 1 GPA	3,704	2.65	
Algebra 2 GPA	3,704	2.25	
1992 NELS			
Total academic GPA	4,988	2.28	−0.19
Algebra 1 GPA	4,988	2.44	−0.21
Algebra 2 GPA	4,988	2.06	−0.19

Table 5.3

**Mean Math GPAs of Students Who Took Algebra
and Advanced Math**

	N	Mean	Difference, NEL–HSB
1982 HSB			
Total academic GPA	552	2.98	
Algebra 1 GPA	552	3.16	
Algebra 2 GPA	552	2.93	
Advanced math GPA	552	2.83	
1992 NELS			
Total academic GPA	841	2.66	–0.32
Algebra 1 GPA	841	2.83	–0.33
Algebra 2 GPA	841	2.56	–0.37
Advanced math GPA	841	2.59	–0.24

Estimates of Grading Changes Independent of Scores and Coursework

The correlation of grades with tested proficiency was estimated by comparing the slopes of the regression of academic mathematics GPA on our linked test scores, after adjusting for differences in the reliability of the HSB and NELS tests, as described in Appendix E.

Mean shifts in grades were estimated with a series of models. The first stage simply reestimated raw differences in grades, holding neither scores nor coursework constant. This provides the same information as is shown in the descriptive analyses above but provides an estimate that is internally consistent with subsequent models. The second stage added controls for test scores, and the third added controls for coursework as well. We did not estimate models that included coursework but not scores. We used hierarchical linear models rather than simple regressions to take into account the clustered sampling used in HSB and NELS. These models are described in Appendix D.

Although mean shifts are the more common notion of grade inflation, we present the analysis of correlations first in this section because the results of that analysis influenced the analysis of mean shifts.

The models employed for this analysis are simplifications and have substantial weaknesses that could not be avoided given the limitations of the HSB and NELS data. One weakness is the nature of the tests used. Ideally, one would want to adjust each course grade for proficiency in the specific material that should enter into that grade. For example, one would want to know how geometry grades had changed after controlling for proficiency in geometry. The survey assessments used in NELS and HSB have insufficient coverage of specific course-level domains and necessarily include material irrelevant to any specific course. It is likely, however, that if appropriate tests were available, they would correlate highly with the NELS and HSB tests.

A second weakness is that course labels are at best a very rough indicator of the actual content and level of demand of courses. The fact that two courses were labeled "algebra 1," for example, does not necessarily mean that they covered similar ranges of material or that they covered any given material at similar levels of depth and complexity. In addition, as the percentage of students taking certain courses changed, the mix of those courses may also have changed. For example, if more lower-performing students start taking a course with a given title, one result might be more classes at a relatively easy level. Thus, our controls for changes in coursework are only approximate.

Correlation of Grades with Tested Proficiency

There is no evidence of decreased-correlation grade inflation between the 1982 HSB and the 1992 NELS. Indeed, the correlation between tested proficiency and academic mathematics GPA (disattenuated for unreliability in θ) *increased* from 0.47 in HSB to 0.58 in NELS. It is important to note that this difference in correlations may have been influenced by differences between the HSB and NELS tests that were not addressed by linking. For example, the NELS tests, being adaptive and therefore longer in the aggregate, might have included more content that is directly pertinent to course grades, which could have increased the correlation. However, given the appreciable observed increase in the correlation, it seems unlikely that the use of stronger and identical tests would have reversed the finding and produced an appreciable decrease in the relationship.

Raw Shift in Grades

The first-stage model estimated a trivial increase in mean grades. The estimated mean increase in academic mathematics GPA was 0.02 on the 0–4.3 scale, half the size of the very small change noted in the descriptive analysis presented above.

Changes in Grades Holding Scores Constant

Because the slope of the regression of mathematics grades on test scores changed between the two cohorts, the model that includes test scores as a predictor of grades is necessarily interactive. That is, there is no single estimate of the mean change; the mean change varies depending on the level of tested proficiency.

Our model shows grade *deflation* in mathematics that was larger for students with lower test scores. For most of the range of test scores (specifically, until nearly a full standard deviation above the mean), students with a given test score had *lower* mean grades in NELS than in HSB (Figure 5.7). This difference was appreciable for students who scored below the grand mean on the tests. For students at the mean score (centered $\theta = 0$), the average academic mathematics grade was estimated to be 0.16 lower in NELS than in HSB. For students scoring a standard deviation below the mean test score, the difference in average grades was 0.35. Adjusted grades were equal in the two cohorts for students with scores roughly 0.9 standard deviations above the mean and were higher in NELS for students with scores above that. Note that the difference in slopes between HSB and NELS is slightly exaggerated by differences in reliability. That does not affect the finding of grade deflation, although it presumably slightly biases upward the estimate of that effect for low-scoring students.

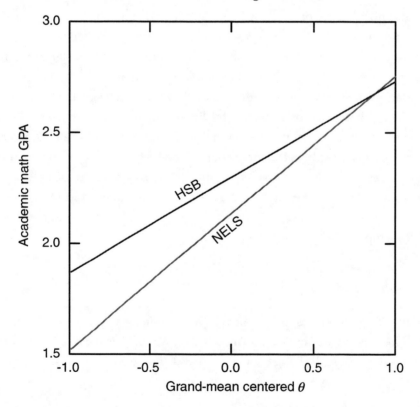

Figure 5.7—Grades as a Function of Test Scores, 1982 HSB and 1992 NELS

Changes in Grades Holding Scores and Coursework Constant

Adding controls for changes in the mix of coursework did not alter the finding that mathematics grades were deflated for many students. The estimated amount of deflation was slightly smaller when coursework was taken into account: 0.14 GPA points at the mean score (Figure 5.8). Controlling for coursework also reduced slightly the difference between HSB and NELS in the slope of the relationship between test scores and grades. As a result, the estimated amount of deflation shrank a bit more (to 0.28) for students one standard deviation below the mean than for students at the mean. Similarly, the point at which estimated deflation was zero increased slightly, to about one standard deviation above the mean.

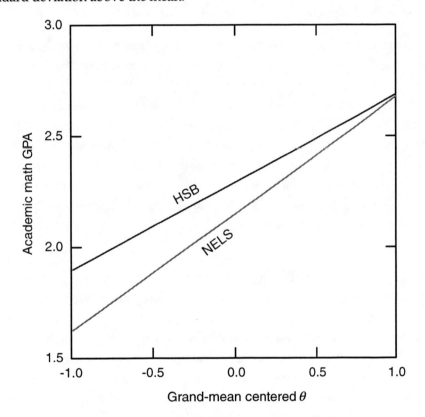

Figure 5.8—Grades as a Function of Test Scores Holding Coursework Constant, 1982 HSB and 1992 NELS

6. A Detailed Look at Predictors of Grades in 1982 and 1992

To understand the influences on grades more fully, we analyzed the relationships between academic mathematics GPA and a variety of student and school characteristics. Identical analyses were carried out in the 1982 and 1992 cohorts. These analyses were two-level hierarchical linear models, with students as level 1 observations and schools as level 2. Additional details of these models can be found in Appendix D.

These analyses were carried out in several stages. The first stage included 11 student-level variables: mathematics score (θ, grand mean centered within cohort), gender, mother's education, four variables indicating the proportion of the student's mathematics grades that came from each of the four categories described previously, and dummy variables for low income, African American, Hispanic, and college-preparatory-track flag. This first-stage model initially included 13 level-2 variables: the school means of each of the 11 student-level variables and flags for rural and urban school location. The location flags were deleted, however, because of a lack of predictive power, so all school-level variables in the analyses reported here are simply the school means of student-level variables.

At this first stage, the relationships between the student-level variables and GPA were held constant across schools. The models were designed to indicate the extent of context effects—that is, the predictive power of school-level variables after controlling for student-level characteristics. For example, a zero coefficient for schools' proportion African American enrollment would not indicate that this proportion fails to predict mean GPA; rather, it would mean that the proportion African American enrollment adds no information beyond that provided by the race and ethnicity of the individual students in the schools.[1]

Because the relationships between scores and grades might vary as a function of student or school characteristics, the second and third stages of analysis entered interactions with scores. The second stage added interactions between students' scores and some other student-level variables, such as the interaction between

---

[1]Specifically, the analysis at stage 1 used fixed-coefficient models and did not center student-level variables around the school means. See Appendix D.

gender and test scores as predictors of GPA. The third stage allowed certain student-level relationships to vary across schools as a function of school characteristics; that is, they added selected cross-level interactions with scores, such as the interaction between students' scores and the percentage of the school's students who self-identified as African American. Some terms that did not significantly predict GPA were removed.

The models described here all included mathematics test scores and thus estimate the relationships between other factors and grades after controlling for tested proficiency in mathematics. However, as noted above, these tests are only limited proxies for the ideal assessments that would measure the proficiencies relevant to the mathematics grades students received. For this reason, caution is needed in interpreting the results of these models. For example, all of the analyses show that holding constant all else in the models, female students received substantially higher mathematics grades than did males. This does not necessarily indicate that teachers applied more lenient grading standards to female students. It is possible that female students on average performed better on aspects of mathematics that were not tested in these assessments but were relevant to their grades. Research has also shown that many teachers consider factors other than proficiency, such as effort and behavior, in assigning grades, and it is possible that female students on average perform better in terms of these factors. It is also plausible, however, that differences in grading standards contributed to the relationships estimated in these models. For example, differences in leniency could have contributed to the relationship between gender and grades, and it is entirely plausible that differences in grading standards among schools of different types contributed to some of the relationships between school characteristics and mean grades.

Although some differences between the findings for the 1982 and 1992 cohorts did appear, the results of the models were generally similar, indicating that the determinants of grades had not changed markedly during the decade between the cohorts. Therefore, to simplify presentation, we focus primarily on results from HSB and then point out some differences that emerged when identical models were run in NELS.

Influences on Grades in 1982 HSB

All of the models showed that scores on the HSB and NELS mathematics tests were moderately strong predictors of grades. In the case of HSB 1982—which showed a weaker relationship between scores and grades than did NELS 1992— each standard deviation increase in test scores predicted an increase of 0.42 in

GPA, on a 0–4.3 scale (Table 6.1). Note that this estimate, which controls for differences on the other variables in this model, is approximately equal to the raw relationship between scores and grades.

The simplest model, from the first stage described above, shows that after test scores are controlled, a number of student- and school-level variables have substantial relationships with academic mathematics GPA. As noted, female students had mean grades exceeding those of males by 0.3 on a 0–4.3 scale (Table 6.1). Both low-income students and students in the college-preparatory track received slightly higher average grades, but these differences, although statistically significant, were very small. The mean grades of Hispanic and African American students were slightly lower than those of other students, but the first of these differences was not significant. (Note that in these models,

Table 6.1

Two-Level (Fixed Coefficients) Model of Academic Mathematics GPA, 1982 HSB

Variable	Estimate	t	p
Student-level variables			
Intercept	2.10	23.8	<0.0001
Female	0.30	16.0	<0.0001
Mother's education	−0.01	−1.9	0.0604
Low income	0.07	2.8	0.0054
Hispanic	−0.05	−1.6	0.1038
African American	−0.08	−2.1	0.0333
Math θ	0.42	30.1	<0.0001
College prep	0.08	3.5	0.0004
Proportion advanced	0.47	3.9	<0.0001
Proportion algebra 1	−0.45	−11.4	<0.0001
Proportion algebra 2	0.32	5.6	<0.0001
Proportion geometry	−0.31	−5.4	<0.0001
School-level variables			
School proportion female	−0.13	−1.7	0.0954
School mean mother's education	0.00	0.2	0.8644
School proportion low income	0.25	3.2	0.0016
School proportion Hispanic	−0.17	−2.0	0.0465
School proportion African American	−0.39	−4.5	<0.0001
School mean math θ	−0.18	−4.0	<0.0001
School proportion college prep	−0.20	−2.6	0.0099
School proportion advanced	−0.32	−1.0	0.3152
School proportion algebra 1	0.55	4.8	<0.0001
School proportion algebra 2	0.28	1.9	0.0603
School proportion geometry	0.30	1.8	0.0766
Residual variances			
τ (between-school)	0.08	11.1	<0.0001
σ^2 (within-school)	5.09	56.3	<0.0001

Hispanic and African American students are compared only to non-Hispanic whites.)

The mix of mathematics courses students took had a strong effect on math GPA, but these effects are hard to interpret. Recall that these variables indicate the proportion of grades derived from courses in each category, with courses fitting into none of the categories (41 percent of grades in HSB and 27 percent in NELS) as the omitted group. The larger the proportion of grades from geometry or algebra 1, the lower the mathematics GPA; the larger the proportion from algebra 2 or advanced classes, the higher the mathematics GPA (Table 6.1). These differences could reflect a mix of selection effects (i.e., differences among the students who enroll in different classes), grading standards, and the correlations between scores on the HSB test and proficiency with the material upon which grades are based on each type of course.

A number of school characteristics showed substantial relationships to mean GPA, even after taking student characteristics into account. Mean test scores and the proportion of students in the college-preparatory track both had significant *negative* relationships to mean GPA, which might indicate tougher grading standards in high-achieving schools (Table 6.1). However, these effects were small. The coefficient for school mean math θ, for example, indicates that an increase of a full standard deviation in mean test scores predicts a decrease of 0.18 in mean GPA, and a school with all students in the college-preparatory track, if one were to exist, would have a mean GPA 0.20 lower than a school that had no students in that track but was otherwise comparable. Consistent with a simpler study of NELS (U.S. Department of Education, 1994), schools with a higher proportion of low-income students had higher mean grades, holding all else constant, but schools with larger Hispanic or especially large African American enrollments had lower mean grades. The proportion African American enrollment had a sizable effect; the model predicts that the mean GPA in an all–African American school would be 0.39 lower than in a school that had no African American enrollment but was otherwise similar. The means of the proportion of marks from each category of courses showed sizable relationships to mean GPA, but only one of these effects was unambiguously significant. That is, the mean proportion of grades from algebra 1 classes showed a strong positive relationship with mean GPA, even though at the student level, students' proportion of grades from this type of class was negatively related to GPA.

The second-stage analysis examined student-level interactions between mathematics test score and four dummy variables that identified students as female, low-income, African American, or Hispanic. This showed that there was no interaction with the African American variable—i.e., the student-level relationship between scores and GPA was essentially the same for African Americans and students who were neither African American nor Hispanic (Table 6.2). There were small interactions with the other three variables, however. The relationship between scores and GPA was slightly stronger for females than for males and slightly weaker for both Hispanics and low-income students. In the language used in the previous section, at the student level, GPA was somewhat more sensitive to tested proficiency for female students and somewhat less sensitive for Hispanic and low-income students.

To start the third stage of the analysis, we allowed the student-level relationship between scores and GPA to vary rather than constraining it to be constant across schools. This variance component was statistically significant, so we attempted to predict the variation among schools using three characteristics of schools: the proportions of students who were African American, Hispanic, or low income.

The only cross-level interaction that was statistically significant was the interaction between mathematics θ and the proportion of students who are low income (Table 6.3). This interaction showed that the student-level relationship between scores and GPA was stronger in schools that had a larger proportion of low-income students. This finding was only marginally significant, however, and it was not replicated in NELS (see below), so it may not warrant interpretation.

Table 6.2

Student-Level Interactions in Prediction of Academic Mathematics GPA, 1982 HSB

Student-Level Interaction	Estimate	t	p
Female $\times$ math θ	0.06	0.01921	0.002
African American $\times$ math θ	−0.01	0.03547	0.71
Hispanic $\times$ math θ	−0.08	0.0315	0.009
Low income $\times$ math θ	−0.10	0.02438	<0.0001

Table 6.3

Cross-Level Interactions in Prediction of Academic Mathematics GPA, 1982 HSB

Cross-Level Interaction	Estimate	t	p
School proportion low income $\times$ math θ	0.14	2.0	0.047
School proportion African American $\times$ math θ	−0.09	−1.4	0.165
School proportion Hispanic $\times$ math θ	−0.08	−1.1	0.267

Influences on Grades in 1992 NELS

The simple two-level model in NELS showed the same general patterns as the comparable model in HSB, but the size of some estimates differed. The discussion here focuses on the differences. In the following tables, a column showing the differences in estimates between the two cohorts has been added, and variables for which estimates changed appreciably and significant are in shaded rows.

Several of the estimates of student-level relationships changed appreciably between 1982 and 1992. As noted above, the relationship between test scores and mathematics GPA became stronger (Table 6.4)—by 0.10, when holding all else in

Table 6.4

Two-Level (Fixed Coefficients) Model of Academic Mathematics GPA, 1992 NELS

Variable	Estimate	t	p	Difference, NELS–HSB
Student-level variables				
Intercept	2.03	27.4	<0.0001	–0.07
Female	0.21	12.9	<0.0001	–0.08
Mother's education	0.01	1.3	0.1863	0.02
Low income	0.04	2.0	0.0488	–0.02
Hispanic	–0.07	–1.7	0.089	–0.02
African American	–0.09	–2.6	0.0096	–0.01
Math θ	0.52	32.8	<0.0001	0.10
College prep	0.13	6.7	<0.0001	0.05
Proportion advanced	0.64	6.0	<0.0001	0.16
Proportion algebra 1	–0.70	–12.6	<0.0001	–0.25
Proportion algebra 2	0.30	5.4	<0.0001	–0.02
Proportion geometry	–0.57	–8.9	<0.0001	–0.25
School-level variables				
School proportion female	–0.11	–2.1	0.0398	0.02
School mean mother's education	0.04	2.2	0.0279	0.03
School proportion low income	0.19	2.8	0.0048	–0.06
School proportion Hispanic	–0.11	–1.5	0.1242	0.06
School proportion African American	–0.27	–4.1	<0.0001	0.11
School mean math θ	–0.14	–3.5	0.0005	0.03
School proportion college prep	–0.16	–3.0	0.0032	0.03
School proportion advanced	–0.45	–1.5	0.1449	–0.13
School proportion algebra 1	0.54	3.9	0.0001	–0.02
School proportion algebra 2	0.39	2.9	0.0042	0.11
School proportion geometry	0.33	2.0	0.047	0.03
Residual variances				
τ (between-school)	0.10	14.1	<0.0001	0.02
σ^2 (within-school)	3.20	54.3	<0.0001	–1.88

the model constant. Both the positive association between GPA and the proportion of grades from advanced courses and the negative associations between GPA and the proportion of grades from algebra 1 and geometry became substantially stronger. The cause of this change is not clear. The gender difference in grades shrank somewhat.

Two changes in school-level relationships stand out. First, the association between high proportions of African American students and lower mean GPA became substantially weaker between 1982 and 1992 (Table 6.4). Second, the positive relationship between mean GPA and the mean proportion of grades from algebra 2 classes became stronger.

Student-level interactions between test scores and gender, race/ethnicity, and income remained small in NELS, and none was highly significant (Table 6.5). The one substantial cross-level interaction that appeared in HSB, test scores by school proportion low income, vanished in NELS (Table 6.6).

Table 6.5

Student-Level Interactions in Prediction of Academic Mathematics GPA, 1992 NELS

Student-Level Interaction	Estimate	t	p	Difference, NELS–HSB
Female $\times$ math θ	0.08	3.9	<0.0001	0.02
African American $\times$ math θ	−0.05	−1.5	0.1442	−0.04
Hispanic $\times$ math θ	−0.02	−0.6	0.5851	0.06
Low income $\times$ math θ	−0.06	−2.3	0.0207	0.04

Table 6.6

Cross-Level Interactions in Prediction of Academic Mathematics GPA, 1992 NELS

Cross-Level Interaction	Estimate	t	p	Difference, NELS–HSB
School proportion low income $\times$ math θ	−0.02	−0.3	0.7892	−0.16
School proportion African American $\times$ math θ	−0.12	−2.1	0.0398	−0.03
School proportion Hispanic $\times$ math θ	−0.03	−0.4	0.6895	0.05

7. Discussion

Taken together, the results presented here are largely inconsistent with anecdotal reports of serious grade inflation in high school. We distinguished between two types of grade inflation: a mean shift, in which the average grades of students at a given level of proficiency increase, and decreased correlation, in which the relationship between grades and tested proficiency weakens. Neither type of grade inflation was apparent in our analyses.

Descriptive analyses showed increases between 1982 and 1992 in both the mean overall GPA of high school seniors and in the percentage of grades greater than or equal to B, but in most instances, these increases were very small. More detailed analysis of academic mathematics grades casts further doubt on the existence of large-scale grade inflation. Course grades for subsamples with comparable levels of mathematics courses dropped from 1982 to 1992, perhaps reflecting a decrease in the selectivity of those courses stemming from the large increase in the proportion of students enrolling in them. Tested proficiency in mathematics increased substantially during the decade in question, and if this increase is taken into account, adjusted grades actually decreased, particularly for low-scoring students. Taking into account the sizable increases in mathematics coursework in general and in advanced coursework in particular only slightly lessened the estimated grade deflation. In mathematics, the correlation of GPA with tested proficiency increased from 1982 to 1992. Finally, multilevel models of the predictors of grades showed relatively modest changes from 1982 to 1992.

The limitations of these analyses are important and need to be considered in interpreting these findings. One important set of limitations stems from the achievement tests used. Ideally, an analysis of changes in grading standards would control for students' mastery of the material that should count toward each grade. In mathematics, for example, the ideal would be to have a test for algebra 1, another test for algebra 2, and so on, each linked across two cohorts. We did not have access to so much detail about student achievement. Rather, we had only the general-purpose survey tests administered with the HSB and NELS surveys. Therefore, our controls for student achievement are incomplete, and better controls might have yielded substantially different estimates of adjusted changes in grading. Moreover, even though the HSB and NELS mathematics tests were linked using accepted methods, they are not equivalent. It is possible, for example, that the NELS test, which is adaptive (i.e., it employs different forms for students at different levels of proficiency), is a better measure of the material relevant to certain course grades than is the HSB test. If this were so, it could explain the increased correlation of grades with scores in NELS, and it could also have affected our estimates of adjusted changes in grading.

The available measures of coursework are similarly insufficient. At any one time, there can be a great deal of variation in content and difficulty within each of the course categories we used, such as "algebra 1" and "geometry." More threatening to our analyses is the fact that there could be differences across time as well. For example, as the mean number of mathematics courses increased and the percentage of students taking relatively advanced courses grew, the typical content or difficulty level of a given type of course could have changed in response. Thus, our controls for changes in course-taking are also less than ideal.

Nonetheless, the consistency of our results across different types of analysis strongly suggests that there was no large-scale, substantial grade inflation, at least in mathematics, between 1982 and 1992. Better measures and models could lead to somewhat different estimates, but it seems unlikely that they would lead to a dramatically different finding.

If these conclusions are correct, what accounts for their inconsistency with widespread and persuasive accounts of serious grade inflation? There are several possible explanations, all of which are only speculative. One is that grade inflation has occurred in recent years but happened primarily outside the time period considered here—either before or after the cohorts graduating between 1982 and 1992. This hypothesis is consistent with the findings of Ziomek and Svec (1995), who found minor inflation from 1990 through 1992 but more substantial inflation later. Analyses now under way at the College Board are also consistent with this hypothesis and have found evidence of grade inflation occurring after the period we considered.[1] A second possibility is that localized increases in grades attracted great attention and created an impression of changes more pervasive than those that actually occurred. For example, we did find a small increase in mean overall GPA and a more sizable increase in mathematics GPA among high-income students. Grade inflation in some high-income schools might have attracted the attention of both the press and of universities that draw disproportionately from schools serving advantaged youth. A third possibility is that grading standards in earlier years were not as stringent as many people recall them to be and that instances of overly lenient

---

[1]Personal communication from W. Camara, E. Kimmel, and J. Scheuneman, 2000.

grading are not a new phenomenon. Grades may have been higher than people remember, and the work corresponding to a given grade might not have been easier than it is now. Indeed, in one of the authors' communities, for example, it is common to hear parents commenting that their children are required to do much harder work in high school than the parents had to do a generation earlier.

Possible changes in grading standards remain an important issue, however. This possibility is of critical importance to postsecondary institutions, and it is also a key concern for K–12 educators in an era in which the enforcement of standards is a central focus of education policy. Therefore, further exploration is warranted. For example, it is important to explore whether grade inflation occurred outside the period covered by this study. Other types of research would be an important complement to the type of work presented here. Research that uses large-scale surveys and the general-purpose achievement tests that are typically administered in them provide a coarse lens. Such research is useful for discerning large-scale trends and some of the rudimentary relationships that accompany them but is not fully sufficient to explore changes in grading standards. Other types of research that sacrifice scale and perhaps representativeness for the sake of greater detail may provide a necessary complement. For example, some states and districts administer end-of-course examinations that would be far stronger than the tests used here as controls for student mastery of grade-related content. Similarly, detailed examination of students admitted to specific postsecondary institutions might provide evidence of changes in the level of preparedness of accepted students with a given level of GPA.

A. IRT Scaling of Mathematics Test Scores, 1982 HSB Seniors and 1992 NELS Seniors

by Thomas Sullivan

Response Matrix

The first step was to create a matrix of item responses (and corresponding answer key) for the test-taking students in each cohort. All students who responded to at least one question, had a positive questionnaire weight (F2QWT for NELS or FUWT for HSB), and had been administered the test (TESTFLAG = 1) were used in the scaling regardless of their presence in our final analysis of grading standards. IRT calibration was based on a weighted response vector where the weights are derived from (1) the test weight (a rescaled test weight for NELS that forced strata weight totals to be the same for the questionnaire students and the test-taking students), and (2) the follow-up test weight, FUTESTWT, for HSB. The rescaled weights used are k_i times the original test weights ($i = 1, 2$), where k_i is a cohort-specific scalar that forces the sum of the weights in both cohorts to be the same (and therefore to contribute equally to the scaling).

Groups

In total, there are 94 unique mathematics items across the two cohorts, i.e., HSB and NELS seniors. There are 38 questions in the HSB test, 70 questions in the NELS tests, and 14 items common to both ($70 + 38 - 14 = 94$). Different NELS tests were administered to three ability groups (low, medium, and high). For purposes of the IRT analysis, each of these different test forms defines a test-taking "group."

IRT Item Parameter Estimation

BILOG-MG was used with marginal maximum likelihood (MML) estimation of the item parameters and maximum likelihood estimation of the θ distribution. Separate prior distributions on the θ vectors were allowed for each of the four groups during the item calibration phase but a common set of item parameters was estimated for all students regardless of their group. To solve the indeterminacy of the location of the θ vectors, the first group (HSB) was used as reference and that ability vector was rescaled to follow an N(0, 1) distribution. Beta prior distributions were put on the guessing parameter of each item so that the mean was equal to 1/k where k is the number of possible responses. Since the mean of a β prior is $a/(a - \beta)$ and the variance is $a\beta/[(a + \beta)^2(a + \beta + 1)]$, any a can be arbitrarily chosen for a fixed β to get the desired prior mean. However, to control the variance subject to a target mean, the sum of $a + \beta$ must be carefully chosen. BILOG-MG initially chooses the values so that $a + \beta = 20$, and our priors reflected the same approach. The prior means are determined by the number of possible responses (3, 4, or 5). Prior means and standard deviations for the slope assume a lognormal distribution and are set to mean (a) = 1, SD(a) = 1.649.

For the first round of estimates, 25 iterations were run and convergence to the default tolerance was not achieved. However, this was an exploratory run to see if more informative priors were needed on the item parameters.

Contributions to the IRT literature (Hambleton, 1989; Lord, 1975; Thissen and Wainer, 1985; de Gruijter, 1984; Swaminathan and Gifford, 1986) suggest that informative priors should be attached to item parameters if (a) the slope is large (at least 2.0) and (b) the value $b_i - 2/a_i < -k$ where b_i is the estimated threshold (difficulty) for item i, a_i is the estimated slope (discrimination) for item i, and k is some positive constant (Lord suggests k = 4 for large samples). Using these guidelines, we attached a prior to the guessing parameters of items 2 and 88, and to the slopes of items 56 and 89. The guessing parameter priors are accomplished by attaching beta distribution parameters so that the prior mean is 1/2k while maintaining the restriction that $a + \beta = 20$. For the slope priors, the mean was again set to 1 but the standard deviation was set to a value much smaller than the default (0.085 instead of 1.645) to keep the slope estimate from wandering off to a large number. In this multiparameter estimation, the likelihood surface may have many local maxima, and the goal is to initialize the calibration at a point in the likelihood surface that returns values consistent with historical IRT results.

After imposing these priors and increasing the number of iterations to 50, a new BILOG file was created for a second calibration. However, it should be noted that the attached priors on the slopes resulted in their new estimates actually being higher (an unexplainable phenomena in BILOG that should not occur with extremely strong priors). So, a third calibration was run that just attached the priors to the guessing parameters. Unfortunately, the results were contrary to the intervention and so we returned to the original estimation without intervention, but now increasing the iterations to 50.

Using the results of this calibration, maximum likelihood estimation of the θ distribution was conducted while holding the item parameters fixed at their estimated values. The score vector was then rescaled so that the weighted scores, without regard to group membership, would have an N(0, 1) distribution. The rescaling transformation preserves the Number Right True Score (NRTS) values that were available before the rescaling by modifying the a_i, b_i, and θ values.

The weighted values of θ for each group are shown in Table A.1 and Figure A.1.

Table A.1

Weighted θ

Cohort	Test	N	Mean	SD	Minimum	Maximum
Both		39,926	0.00	1.00	–3.82	3.37
HSB	All	25,690	–0.15	1.06	–3.82	3.37
NELS	All	14,236	0.15	0.91	–2.25	2.84
NELS	NELS low	2,554	–0.77	0.53	–2.25	0.75
NELS	NELS medium	7,717	0.06	0.71	–2.20	2.34
NELS	NELS high	3,965	1.21	0.51	–0.45	2.84

Number Right True Scores and Number Right Formula Scores

The vector of θ values can be passed through the item parameters from the HSB test (i = 1,. . . . , 38 items) or the NELS test (i = 1, . . . , 70 items) to get an expected probability of answering item i correctly for student n (n = 1, . . . , N), which will be called $P_i^{(n)}(\theta)$. The number right true score for the nth student is $\sum_i P_i^{(n)}(\theta)$. For each student, we computed a NRTS using the HSB scores (H_NRTS) and the NELS (N_NRTS) scores. To get the Number Right Formula Scores (NRFS) for the HSB test, we used H_NRFS = H-NRTS – (38 – H_NRTS)/3, where 38 is the number of items and 3 is the number of alternatives minus 1. Similarly, a NRFS was computed for NELS (N_NRFS), but 70 and 3.328571 (the mean number of responses – 1) were used in the transformation.

Note that all 70 item parameters were used for assigning NRTS and NRFS to students with NELS parameters even though each NELS student was administered only 40 of the 70 questions depending on his or her ability group. It is possible to construct a set of scores based only on each test form, but data exploration suggested this was unnecessary. Table A.2 is a summary of the estimated NRFS values by test form. The correlations of the NRFS in Table A.3 show that the estimates are stable regardless of the item parameters used.

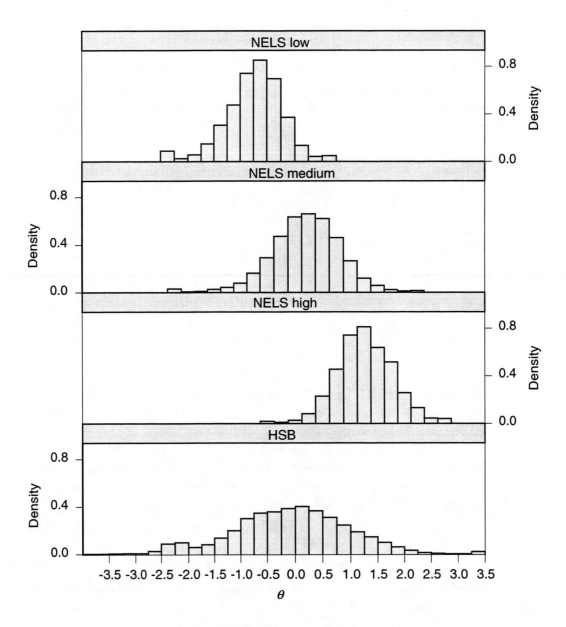

Figure A.1—Distributions of θ by Group

Figure A.2 shows the NRTS by actual number of items answered correctly (jittered) by test form and cohort. One would expect the two NRTS and actual number of items answered correctly to have a strong positive correlation. One would also expect the estimates to be more stable as the number of correct items approaches 38 since, in lower values of "CORRECT," the items answered correctly by each student may be of varying difficulty. But, as n → 38, the correctly answered items become the same for each observation.

Table A.2

NRFS Values by Test Form

Cohort	Test	N	Variable	Label	Mean	SD	Range
HSB	HSB	25,690	PCT_CORR	Percent correct	0.51	0.22	1.00
			H_NRFS	HSB NRFS	13.44	10.78	40.50
			N_NRFS	NELS NRFS	23.54	17.81	75.86
			S_H_NRFS	HSB NRFS standardized	−0.14	1.01	3.78
			S_N_NRFS	NELS NRFS standardized	−0.14	1.02	4.33
			SCALE	θ scaled to weighted N(0,1)	−0.15	1.06	7.19
NELS	NELS high	3,965	PCT_CORR	Percent correct	0.63	0.15	0.88
			H_NRFS	HSB NRFS	28.90	5.05	29.53
			N_NRFS	NELS NRFS	48.66	8.94	52.87
			S_H_NRFS	HSB NRFS standardized	1.30	0.47	2.76
			S_N_NRFS	NELS NRFS standardized	1.29	0.51	3.02
			SCALE	θ scaled to weighted N(0,1)	1.21	0.51	3.29
NELS	NELS medium	7,717	PCT_CORR	Percent correct	0.54	0.16	0.98
			H_NRFS	HSB NRFS	15.36	8.21	38.46
			N_NRFS	NELS NRFS	26.73	13.08	69.87
			S_H_NRFS	HSB NRFS standardized	0.04	0.77	3.59
			S_N_NRFS	NELS NRFS standardized	0.04	0.75	3.99
			SCALE	θ scaled to weighted N(0,1)	0.06	0.71	4.55
NELS	NELS low	2,554	PCT_CORR	Percent correct	0.47	0.14	0.93
			H_NRFS	HSB NRFS	5.48	4.77	26.26
			N_NRFS	NELS NRFS	11.01	8.19	44.77
			S_H_NRFS	HSB NRFS standardized	−0.88	0.45	2.45
			S_N_NRFS	NELS NRFS standardized	−0.86	0.47	2.55
			SCALE	θ scaled to weighted N(0,1)	−0.77	0.53	3.00

Table A.3

Weighted Correlations Among Scales

	PCT_CORR	H_NRFS	N_NRFS	S_H_NRFS	S_N_NRFS	SCALE
PCT_CORR	1.00	0.92	0.92	0.92	0.92	0.91
H_NRFS		1.00	1.00	1.00	1.00	0.97
N_NRFS			1.00	1.00	1.00	0.99
S_H_NRFS				1.00	1.00	0.97
S_N_NRFS					1.00	0.99
SCALE						1.00

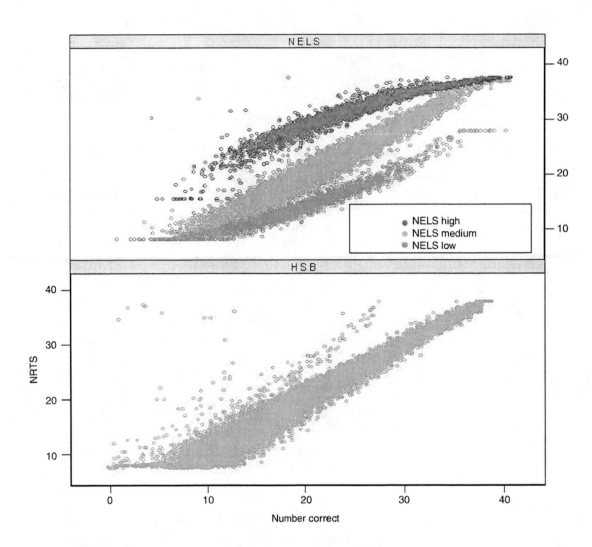

Figure A.2—Number Right True Score by Number Correct, by Group

B. Subsample Noncomparability

The HSB and NELS surveys were intended to represent the population of students in the years of their administration. The degree to which they meet this goal depends on how well they are designed, implemented, and weighted. For example, their design must incorporate a good sampling frame for schools; their implementation must obtain a high rate of response; and the weighting of data must reflect both design factors (e.g., differences in the probability of sampling different types of schools) and rates of nonresponse.

Analysis of the data from these surveys, however, is typically carried out on one or more subsamples of the data. It is useful to think of analysis subsamples as designed and ad hoc. Designed subsamples are addressed in the design of the survey, for example, by creating appropriate weights or by "freshening" a sample to replaced cases lost by attrition. For example, because not all students in NELS and HSB who took the base-year test in each survey took the first follow-up tests, different weights are provided for analyzing the base-year and first-follow-up test data. Ad hoc subsamples arise in the course of carrying out analyses. For example, if one uses two or more variables together in an analysis, missing data on each of the variables will make it necessary to drop some cases, and the remaining subsample may be appreciably different from any subsample for which weights are provided.

Even if the survey is well designed and implemented and appropriately weighted, the subsamples used in analysis may differ enough from the total sample to threaten the validity of findings. These differences may make findings unrepresentative of the population and may bias comparisons between surveys, such as our comparisons between HSB and NELS. We use the term "subsample noncomparability" to refer to these differences between analysis subsamples and the entire sample. Substantial subsample noncomparability may arise when ad hoc sample loss is sizable and nonrandom, and it may also arise when the measures taken in response to design subsample differences, such as freshening, are not sufficient to offset differences between the subsample and the sample.

In longitudinal studies, a primary source of noncomparability is attrition over time, but there are other potentially important sources as well. When surveys are refreshed periodically to offset attrition (as was NELS but not HSB), differences between the freshening sample and the cases lost by attrition may leave noncomparability or even add to it. Both instrument-level and item-level nonresponse can contribute to noncomparability, as can unusable responses.

A standard method for addressing noncomparability is the use of design weights, i.e., weights reflecting the probability of selection in the design and the probability of nonresponse. For example, the differences between the transcript and questionnaire subsamples of NELS are addressed by the use of separate design weights for each subsample, which are intended to make each subsample representative of the population. However, design weights may not be enough to maintain representativeness. Weighting may be insufficient, for example, when nonrandom sample loss occurs within the strata used to define weights. Weighting can also be insufficient when ad hoc subsamples differ substantially from those addressed by weights that are available or can be constructed from other data in the survey database

We had several reasons to be concerned about noncomparability of the analysis samples used here. We used test data from the first follow-up of HSB and the second follow-up of NELS, and in both samples there was considerable attrition by the time of the relevant follow-up data collection. Our analysis required that students have both transcript data and complete follow-up test data. This requirement caused substantial sample loss. Neither the HSB nor the NELS database contained weights specifically designed for this subsample, and neither contained the design weight factors and nonresponse factors needed to construct appropriate analysis weights. Our preliminary tabulations suggested that the students lost from our analysis sample because of the requirement that both test and transcript data be present differed appreciably from those retained. Valerie Lee alerted us to possible problems with the weights assigned to students in the NELS freshening samples.[1]

For our purposes, the primary sources of sample noncomparability were attrition over time and sample loss from our requirement that students have test scores as well as transcripts. This combined loss cannot be assessed with a single comparison, because the students added by freshening lack a base-year test (making it impossible to determine whether they were comparable to the students they replaced in terms of initial achievement), and those lost because of attrition or because of the lack of follow-up testing cannot be compared in terms of performance on the follow-up test. Therefore, the effect of these factors and the adequacy of any particular set of weights had to be determined from a number of different contrasts.

---

[1]Personal communication, March 8, 1999.

This appendix describes the design of the noncomparability analysis, the findings, and the restandardization of weights.

Design of the Noncomparability Analysis

Table B.1 shows the contrasts used to examine the practical impact of sample noncomparability and the variables that could be evaluated for each. For example, the subsamples specified by the first contrast could be evaluated in terms of differences in GPA, demographics, and baseline scores but not in terms of differences in follow-up scores. All four of the contrasts among groups could be evaluated in terms of GPA and demographics, but only the first and fourth contrasts could be evaluated in terms of their effects on scores.

The purposes of the four contrasts are as follows:

1. This contrast looks at combined sample loss from attrition and instrument nonresponse other than follow-up test nonresponse. Nonresponse to the follow-up test is too substantial to be considered here and is evaluated separately. Cases that lack baseline scores or valid GPAs had to be excluded from this contrast.

2. By comparison with contrast 1, this one shows the effect of freshening, without the extra selection criterion of a present follow-up score. Baseline scores cannot be used as an outcome here because the freshening sample lacks them.

Table B.1

Contrasts Used to Test Sample Noncomparability

Samples	GPA	Demo-graphics	Baseline Scores	Follow-Up Scores
1) Base sample vs. transcript sample, no freshening	X	X	X	
2) Base sample vs. transcript sample, with freshening	X	X		
3) Total refreshed transcript sample, total vs. those with follow-up test scores	X	X		
4) Refreshed vs. unrefreshed transcript samples, both with follow-up scores	X	X		X

3. Comparison of this with contrast 2 will show the effect of sample loss from students who lack follow-up tests. We cannot use tests as an outcome because students in the freshening sample cases lack baseline test scores, and many in this group lack follow-up scores.

4. Comparison of this with contrast 2 will show whether imposition of the extra criterion of a present follow-up score undermines the effectiveness of the freshening, and it also allows use of a test score outcome.

Findings

The contrasts above were examined separately for HSB and NELS. The findings shown by HSB and NELS were fundamentally different, but in both cases, the analyses suggested that simply weighting our analysis sample with the transcript-file weights would provide reasonable distributions of test scores and grades.

HSB

Sample loss from the baseline sample to our analysis sample was very large. Only 54 percent of the base-year sample had transcripts, and only 50 percent had both transcripts and follow-up test scores.

The effect of applying the HSB transcript weights is to raise the distribution of GPA slightly. Using the transcript rather than the base-year weights for the subsample with transcripts raises the mean by 0.03 standard deviation. This difference in means suggests that the strata that lost more students going from the base year to transcript samples tend to have *higher* GPA, because weighting with the transcript weights—which should inflate the counts of cells that lost relatively many students—raises mean GPA.

The freshening sample was small but not trivial (7.5 percent of students with transcripts). This small freshening sample has very low GPA and follow-up math scores (roughly –0.4 SD), and its inclusion drops the mean GPA and test scores by 0.05 or 0.06 SD.

Despite the huge sample loss, the subgroup with both test scores and transcripts has a mean base-year mathematics score fairly similar to that of the full base-year math sample—about 0.05 higher after reweighting (that is, comparing the full sample weighted by the base-year weights to the subsample with transcripts weighted by the transcript weights). This necessarily uses the unrefreshed sample. Adding in the freshening sample would drop mean follow-up mathematics scores by nearly 0.06 SD. Thus, one might conclude that the effect of freshening and reweighting, in combination, is likely to leave mean scores about where they were in the base-year sample. This in turn suggests that the GPA distribution of the analysis subsample is probably reasonable.

NELS

Using the transcript rather than the base-year weights for the transcript sample drops the mean GPA by 0.13 standard deviation. This suggests that the strata that lost more students tend to have *lower* GPA, because weighting with the transcript weights—which should inflate the counts of cells that lost relatively many students—lowers mean GPA.

The effect on base-year test scores is in the same direction but smaller. Using the transcript weights rather than base-year weights to tabulate base-year mathematics scores drops mean scores by roughly 0.07 SD.

The effect of freshening on these various means is typically very small, partly because the freshening subsample is so small. Including the freshening sample drops the mean of follow-up mathematics scores by only 0.03 standard deviation.

Freshening did an imperfect job of maintaining the demographic composition of the sample in the face of loss from attrition. The refreshed, reweighted transcript sample has slightly fewer whites and shows a slightly different distribution of parental education than the original sample.

Comparing the base-year mathematics scores for the base year and transcript samples, weighted with their own appropriate weights, shows that the mean for the transcript sample is higher by less than 0.04 SD. The follow-up mathematics contrast between the refreshed and unrefreshed sample noted above suggests that including the freshening students would drop that mean a bit, perhaps 0.02 or 0.03 SD, if we had base-year mathematics scores for them, leaving only a very small difference in base-year mathematics scores. It is probably reasonable to expect a similar effect on GPA. This suggests that the use of the transcript weights on the refreshed sample is reasonable.

Restandardizing the Transcript Weights

The average sampling weight is large because the weights inflate the counts of sampled individuals to match the estimated population. For our purposes, however, this inflation of counts was neither necessary nor desirable. It is unnecessary because all of our analyses reflect the relative size of groups rather than their absolute size. It is undesirable because a large ratio of the sum of the weights to the count of sampled individuals can bias the results because of the weighting algorithms used in some commercial software. Accordingly, we first standardized the weights so that the sum of the weights equaled the count of students in the analysis sample. This adjustment created another problem, however: For some groups with relatively small weights, variance estimates became seriously inflated because the term $(\sum w_i - 1)$, where w_i is the weight for individual i, became very small. Accordingly, our final weights were standardized such that $\sum w_i = 10 \cdot \sum N$.

C. Analysis of the Feasibility of Using SAT and ACT Scores as Covariates

Mathematics is the only subject for which we have linked HSB and NELS test scores that permit a control for changes in proficiency when modeling changes in grading standards. Simple raw changes in grade distributions, however, indicated that mathematics may differ from some other subjects in important ways, and mathematics showed relatively little raw change in grades. Accordingly, we carried out a number of analyses to determine whether it would be practical to use SAT or ACT scores to control for differences in proficiency between the 1982 HSB cohort and the 1992 NELS cohort. If SAT or ACT scores could be used in this way, it would be possible to model changes in subjects other than mathematics, because SAT and ACT scores are equated over time.

A principal threat to using SAT and ACT scores as controls for proficiency changes is the possibility that the selectivity of the self-selected subsamples of students who took the tests changed appreciably in ways that might change the relationships between scores and grades. Accordingly, we examined changes in the characteristics of these self-selected groups and changes in the relationships between scores and grades. These analyses suggested that it would be problematic to use SAT or ACT scores in this manner.

The proportion of students taking the SAT, ACT, or both increased sharply between the two cohorts. Roughly 20 percent of students in HSB took each of the tests, and less than 40 percent took one or the other (Table C.1). In contrast, roughly one-third of the students in NELS took each of the tests, and nearly 60 percent took one or the other.

This increase was not uniform across demographic groups. The largest proportional increases in the percentages of students taking both tests was among Native Americans (who constitute a very small percentage of test-takers)

Table C.1

Weighted Proportions of Students Taking
ACT and SAT, HSB and NELS

	Took ACT	Took SAT	Took Either
HSB	0.19	0.21	0.37
NELS	0.32	0.37	0.59

and Hispanics (Table C.2). The percentages of white and Asian students taking the test grew the least. The percentage of African American students taking the test grew somewhat more than that of whites. Thus, the increase in the proportion of students taking the tests stemmed in substantial part from the relatively faster growth in test-taking by historically lower-scoring groups.

It is also important to consider changes in the composition of the test-taking population, which is determined by both the changes in selectivity within groups and the changes in size of the groups. Because the various racial/ethnic groups grew at substantially different rates during the decade between HSB and NELS, changes in the test-taking population were very different from changes in selectivity within groups. The percentage of test-takers who identified themselves as Asian more than doubled (Table C.3), an increase that was offset by much smaller changes in the percentages who identified themselves as either African American or Hispanic. The percentage of test-takers who identified themselves as white stayed nearly constant.

Table C.2

Percentage and Change in Percentage of Students Taking ACT and SAT by Race/Ethnicity, HSB and NELS

	Race/Ethnicity	% Taking ACT	% Taking SAT	% Taking Either
HSB	Native American	12	9	20
	Asian	12	35	45
	African American	9	15	24
	Hispanic	9	12	20
	White	22	24	41
NELS	Native American	18	29	45
	Asian	26	55	66
	African American	21	28	44
	Hispanic	21	30	43
	White	36	38	64
Difference, NELS–HSB	Native American	7	21	25
	Asian	14	20	21
	African American	12	13	21
	Hispanic	11	18	23
	White	14	15	23
Percentage change, HSB to NELS	Native American	58	244	126
	Asian	115	59	48
	African American	128	85	86
	Hispanic	120	149	117
	White	65	63	55

Table C.3

**Weighted Composition of Groups Taking ACT and SAT
by Race/Ethnicity, HSB and NELS**

	Race/Ethnicity	% Taking ACT	% Taking SAT	% Taking Either
HSB	Native American	0.01	0.01	0.01
	Asian	0.02	0.05	0.04
	African American	0.07	0.10	0.10
	Hispanic	0.12	0.12	0.12
	White	0.78	0.72	0.74
NELS	Native American	0.01	0.01	0.01
	Asian	0.06	0.11	0.08
	African American	0.06	0.06	0.06
	Hispanic	0.07	0.09	0.08
	White	0.81	0.74	0.77
Difference, NELS–HSB	Native American	0.00	0.00	0.00
	Asian	0.04	0.06	0.04
	African American	–0.02	–0.04	–0.03
	Hispanic	–0.05	–0.04	–0.04
	White	0.03	0.02	0.03
Percentage change, HSB to NELS	Native American	–48	14	–19
	Asian	194	118	117
	African American	–24	–38	–33
	Hispanic	–39	–31	–35
	White	4	3	5

When students are classified by their mother's highest level of educational attainment, differences in selectivity changes were more modest but still appreciable. The percentage of students taking either college admissions test increased in all groups, from a low of 35 percent to a high of 72 percent (Table C.4). However, these percentage changes do not show a consistent pattern across educational groups.

Coupled with changes in maternal educational attainment, these changes in selectivity produced a substantial change in the educational profile of the families of test-takers. The percentage of test-takers whose mothers had at least a college education increased substantially, whereas the percentage of students from most other educational groups dropped to offset this (Table C.5).

Changes in selectivity also varied substantially but inconsistently among income groups. The largest increase was among students in the lowest income category, but the pattern is otherwise inconsistent (Table C.6). The income distribution among families with children changed considerably over the decade, however, and the result was a more striking change in the income distribution of students

Table C.4

Percentage and Change in Percentage of Students Taking ACT and SAT by Mother's Education, HSB and NELS

	Mother's Education	% Taking ACT	% Taking SAT	% Taking Either
HSB	Less than high school	11	11	21
	Trade/vocational	18	23	37
	High school graduate	19	19	36
	Some college	26	28	48
	Finished college	26	41	60
	Master's degree	25	37	56
	Ph.D., M.D., etc.	17	36	49
NELS	Less than high school	17	19	33
	Trade/vocational	33	39	65
	High school graduate	32	31	56
	Some college	33	44	65
	Finished college	37	54	75
	Master's degree	42	58	82
	Ph.D., M.D., etc.	54	66	83
Difference, NELS– HSB	Less than high school	6	8	12
	Trade/vocational	15	16	27
	High school graduate	13	12	20
	Some college	7	16	17
	Finished college	11	13	15
	Master's degree	16	22	26
	Ph.D., M.D., etc.	37	30	34
Percentage change, HSB to NELS	Less than high school	58	70	58
	Trade/vocational	80	72	72
	High school graduate	71	61	57
	Some college	29	56	35
	Finished college	42	31	26
	Master's degree	64	59	48
	Ph.D., M.D., etc.	226	83	70

taking college admissions tests. The percentage of test-takers from the top income group increased by 44 percent, whereas the percentage from all other groups stayed constant or declined (Table C.7).

These changes in selectivity were accompanied by appreciable changes in the relationships between scores on these tests and high school grades, and these changes were inconsistent between the SAT and ACT. The correlation between SAT-I math scores and the math GPA measures dropped between HSB and NELS, from 0.55 to 0.43 in the case of academic GPA (Table C.8, shaded cells). In the same subsample of students, the correlation between the linked HSB/NELS math θ scores and academic GPA stayed essentially constant, at just below 0.60. In contrast, the correlation between ACT math scores and math GPA

Table C.5

**Weighted Composition of Groups Taking ACT and SAT
by Mother's Education, HSB and NELS**

	Mother's Education	% of ACT Takers	% of SAT Takers	% of Test Takers
HSB	Less than high school	0.11	0.10	0.11
	Trade/vocational	0.10	0.10	0.10
	High school graduate	0.37	0.32	0.35
	Some college	0.20	0.18	0.19
	Finished college	0.14	0.18	0.16
	Master's degree	0.07	0.08	0.07
	Ph.D., M.D., etc.	0.01	0.02	0.02
NELS	Less than high school	0.07	0.06	0.07
	Trade/vocational	0.13	0.12	0.13
	High school graduate	0.35	0.28	0.32
	Some college	0.10	0.11	0.10
	Finished college	0.20	0.24	0.21
	Master's degree	0.12	0.14	0.12
	Ph.D., M.D., etc.	0.04	0.04	0.04
Difference, NELS–HSB	Less than high school	–0.05	–0.04	–0.04
	Trade/vocational	0.03	0.02	0.03
	High school graduate	–0.03	–0.05	–0.03
	Some college	–0.10	–0.07	–0.08
	Finished college	0.06	0.06	0.06
	Master's degree	0.05	0.06	0.05
	Ph.D., M.D., etc.	0.03	0.02	0.02
Percentage change, HSB to NELS	Less than high school	–42	–38	–38
	Trade/vocational	29	21	32
	High school graduate	–7	–14	–9
	Some college	–49	–40	–44
	Finished college	46	33	38
	Master's degree	76	68	68
	Ph.D., M.D., etc.	247	92	92

increased between HSB and NELS, from below 0.50 to above 0.60 (Table C.9, shaded cells). In the ACT subsample, the correlations between the linked HSB/NELS math θ scores and academic GPA also increased.

Given these indications of appreciable and inconsistent selectivity differences for which it would not be feasible to control, we decided not to use the SAT and ACT scores to adjust for differences in proficiency.

Table C.6

Percentage and Change in Percentage of Students Taking ACT and SAT by Income Group, HSB and NELS

	Income Group	% Taking ACT	% Taking SAT	% Taking Either
HSB	1	10	10	20
	2	15	15	29
	3	18	18	33
	4	23	27	45
	5	22	35	50
NELS	1	22	19	37
	2	25	20	40
	3	32	31	56
	4	39	43	69
	5	34	66	82
Difference, NELS–HSB	1	11	8	18
	2	10	5	12
	3	14	14	23
	4	17	16	25
	5	12	31	32
Percentage change, HSB to NELS	1	113	79	89
	2	68	33	40
	3	81	79	70
	4	74	60	55
	5	52	88	64

Table C.7

**Weighted Composition of Groups Taking ACT and SAT
by Income Group, HSB and NELS**

	Income Group	% of ACT Takers	% of SAT Takers	% of Test Takers
HSB	1	0.04	0.04	0.04
	2	0.12	0.10	0.11
	3	0.25	0.22	0.24
	4	0.45	0.46	0.45
	5	0.14	0.19	0.16
NELS	1	0.05	0.03	0.04
	2	0.09	0.06	0.07
	3	0.21	0.18	0.20
	4	0.48	0.44	0.46
	5	0.17	0.28	0.22
Difference, NELS–HSB	1	0.00	0.00	0.00
	2	–0.03	–0.04	–0.04
	3	–0.04	–0.04	–0.04
	4	0.03	–0.01	0.01
	5	0.04	0.10	0.07
Percentage change, HSB to NELS	1	10	–9	4
	2	–27	–43	–35
	3	–16	–18	–16
	4	7	–3	2
	5	26	53	44

Table C.8

**Correlations Between Math GPA and Math Scores, SAT Sample Only (Listwise
Deletion), Weighted (HSB Above Diagonal, NELS Below Diagonal)**

	Academic Math GPA	Overall Math GPA	HSB–NELS Math θ	SAT Math
Academic math GPA	1	0.99	0.57	0.55
Overall math GPA	0.99	1	0.56	0.55
Math θ	0.59	0.59	1	0.82
SAT math	0.43	0.42	0.69	1

NOTE: Correlations disattenuated for measurement error in math θ.

Table C.9

Correlations Between Math GPA and Math Scores, ACT Sample Only (Listwise Deletion), Weighted (HSB Above Diagonal, NELS Below Diagonal)

	Academic Math GPA	Overall Math GPA	HSB–NELS Math θ	ACT Math
Academic math GPA	1	0.98	0.52	0.48
Overall math GPA	0.99	1	0.53	0.48
Math θ	0.61	0.61	1	0.79
ACT math	0.64	0.63	0.82	1

NOTE: Correlations disattenuated for measurement error in math θ.

D. Hierarchical Linear Models Used to Explore the Predictors of Grades

This appendix describes the multilevel models used in Sections 5 and 6.

Section 5

The correlation of grades with tested proficiency was estimated by regressing academic mathematics GPA on our linked test scores, after adjusting for differences in the reliability of the HSB and NELS tests, as described in Appendix E.

Mean shifts in grades were estimated with a series of hierarchical models. These were used instead of simple regression models to account for clustering of students within schools. The first stage simply reestimated raw differences in grades, holding neither scores nor coursework constant. This was done to make the estimates from this series of models internally consistent. The second stage added controls for test scores, and the third added controls for coursework as well. We did not estimate models that included coursework but not scores.

To estimate these models, the NELS and HSB samples were pooled after restandardizing the weights to give the two cohorts equal weight in the pooled sample. Our estimates of θ were centered at the grand mean in the pooled sample.

The base model is a three-level model (students, schools, and cohorts) estimated in the pooled sample. Let Y denote a student's test score, in the restandardized IRT θ metric used throughout this report. Let C indicate cohort, i index students, j index schools, and k index cohorts (0 = HSB, 1 = NELS). Cohort is a fixed effect in all of these models. The base model is then

$$Y_{ijk} = \beta_{0jk} + \varepsilon_{ijk} \tag{D.1}$$

$$\beta_{0jk} = \gamma_{000} + \gamma_{001}C_k + u_{jk} \tag{D.2}$$

$$Y_{ijk} = \gamma_{000} + \gamma_{001}C + u_{jk} + \varepsilon_{ijk} = \gamma_{000} + \gamma_{001}C + r_{ijk} \tag{D.3}$$

where ε_{ijk} is the individual-level random error within schools, u_{jk} is the random error in school means, and r_{ijk} is the random individual-level error in the combined equation.

The second stage adds scores (grand-mean-centered θ) at the student level. The slope of grades on θ differs considerably across the cohorts. Hence this model must include the interaction of cohort with θ.

$$Y_{ijk} = \beta_{0jk} + \beta_{1jk}\theta_{ijk} + \varepsilon_{ijk} \tag{D.4}$$

$$\beta_{0jk} = \gamma_{000} + \gamma_{001}C + u_{jk} \tag{D.5}$$

$$\beta_{1jk} = \gamma_{100} + \gamma_{111}C \tag{D.6}$$

$$Y_{ijk} = \gamma_{000} + \gamma_{001}C + \gamma_{100}\theta_{ijk} + \gamma_{111}C\theta_{ijk} + r_{ijk} \tag{D.7}$$

The slope in Eq. D.6 is fixed because cohort is a fixed effect.

The final stage adds to the previous stage a vector of coursework variables, $\mathbf{X}$. The parameters for these variables are assumed to be fixed. The model is

$$Y_{ijk} = \beta_{0jk} + \beta_{1jk}\theta_{ijk} + \boldsymbol{\beta}'_{200}\,\mathbf{X}_{ijk} + \varepsilon_{ijk} \tag{D.8}$$

$$\beta_{0jk} = \gamma_{000} + \gamma_{001}C + u_{jk} \tag{D.9}$$

$$\beta_{1jk} = \gamma_{100} + \gamma_{111}C \tag{D.10}$$

$$Y_{ijk} = \gamma_{000} + \gamma_{001}C + (\gamma_{100} + \gamma_{111}C)\,\theta_{ijk} + \boldsymbol{\beta}'_{200}\,\mathbf{X}_{ijk} + r_{ijk} \tag{D.11}$$

Section 6

The models described in Section 6 are two-level hierarchical models, with students as level-1 observations and schools as level-2 observations.

Progressively more complex models were constructed and then pared back, based on the apparent importance of specific variables. The initial models were "fixed coefficient" models (Kreft and DeLeeuw, 1998)—that is, the level-1 coefficients were fixed across schools. Subsequent stages entailed allowing the coefficient for student test scores to vary randomly, adding level-1 interactions with scores, and adding cross-level interactions with scores, i.e., variations in level-1 slopes as a function of school characteristics.

Two of the initial variables were "macro" variables, that is, characteristics of schools that are not aggregates of student characteristics. These were dummies for rural and urban school location; both were dropped because they had little predictive power. All other school-level variables were aggregates of student-level variables, and any variable that was included at either level was included in the other.

The initial, fixed-coefficient models can be expressed as follows, where $\mathbf{X_{ij}}$ is a vector of values on predictors $\mathbf{X}$ for individual i in school j, θ_{ij} is the test score of student i in school j, β_1 is the coefficient of test scores, $\boldsymbol{\beta}_2$ is a vector of coefficients for the student-level variables, $\mathbf{Z_j}$ is a vector of values on school-level predictors for school j, $\boldsymbol{\gamma}_1$ is a vector of coefficients for the school-level variables, ε_{ij} and u_j are random error terms in the student and school equations, and r_{ij} is the student-level random error in the combined equation:

$$y_{ij} = \beta_{0j} + \beta_1\theta_{ij} + \boldsymbol{\beta}'_2\mathbf{X_{ij}} + \varepsilon_{ij} \tag{D.12}$$

$$\beta_{0j} = \gamma_{00} + \boldsymbol{\gamma}'_1\mathbf{Z_j} + u_j \tag{D.13}$$

$$y_{ij} = \gamma_{00} + \beta_{1j}\theta_{ij} + \boldsymbol{\beta}'_2\mathbf{X_{ij}} + \boldsymbol{\gamma}'_1\mathbf{Z_j} + r_{ij} \tag{D.14}$$

Once the macro-level variables were dropped, all variables in $\mathbf{Z}$ were the school means of the student-level variables in $\mathbf{X}$. Note that β_1 and all elements of $\boldsymbol{\beta}_2$ are constant across schools and that therefore neither is subscripted with a j in these equations.

The second stage of the analysis allowed the student-level slope of GPA on test scores, β_1, to vary randomly. This model is

$$y_{ij} = \beta_{0j} + \beta_{1j}\theta_{ij} + \boldsymbol{\beta}'_2\mathbf{X_{ij}} + \varepsilon_{ij} \tag{D.15}$$

$$\beta_{0j} = \gamma_{00} + \boldsymbol{\gamma}'_1\mathbf{Z_j} + u_j \tag{D.16}$$

$$\beta_{1j} = \gamma_{10} + u_j^* \tag{D.17}$$

$$y_{ij} = \gamma_{00} + \gamma_{10}\theta_{ij} + \boldsymbol{\beta}'_2\mathbf{X_{ij}} + \boldsymbol{\gamma}'_1\mathbf{Z_j} + r_{ij}^* \tag{D.18}$$

Asterisks are used to differentiate terms from similar terms in differently specified models.

The third stage adds level-1 interactions between scores and selected background variables, $\boldsymbol{\beta}'_3\,\theta_{ij}\,,\mathbf{X_{ij}^*}$, where $\mathbf{X_{ij}^*}$ is the subset of $\mathbf{X_{ij}}$ for which interaction terms were calculated. This makes the combined equation

$$y_{ij} = \gamma_{00} + \gamma_{10}\theta_{ij} + \boldsymbol{\beta}'_2\mathbf{X_{ij}} + \boldsymbol{\beta}'_3\,\theta_{ij}\,\mathbf{X_{ij}^*} + \boldsymbol{\gamma}'_1\mathbf{Z_j} + r_{ij}^{**} \tag{D.19}$$

In the final stage, cross-level interactions between school-level variables and scores were added. That is, the random variation in the student-level slopes on scores in Eq. D.17 was modeled as a function of selected school-level variables $\mathbf{Z_j^*}$:

$$\beta_{1j} = \gamma_{10} + (\boldsymbol{\gamma_2'}\mathbf{Z_j^*}) + u_j^{**} \tag{D.20}$$

This makes the combined equation:

$$y_{ij} = \gamma_{00} + [\gamma_{10} + \boldsymbol{\gamma_2'}\mathbf{Z_j^*}]\theta_{ij} + \boldsymbol{\beta_2'}\mathbf{X_{ij}} + \boldsymbol{\beta_3'}\,\theta_{ij}\,\mathbf{X_{ij}} + \boldsymbol{\gamma_1'}\mathbf{Z_j} + r_{ij}^{***} \tag{D.21}$$

Because a primary purpose of the models was to explore context effects, that is, the effects of school characteristics above and beyond the effects of individual characteristics, none of the student-level variables were centered around their school means. Scores (math θ) was grand mean centered to facilitate the interpretation of interactions.

E. Estimating and Adjusting for Reliability of the HSB and NELS Tests

Comparisons between models estimated using HSB and NELS could be biased by differences in the reliability of the tests used in the two surveys. HSB used a uniform test: All tested individuals in a grade were administered the same form. NELS used adaptive testing, in which students in grades 10 and 12 were administered one of three forms differing in difficulty depending on their performance on the uniform test administered in grade 8. By targeting items more closely to a student's level of proficiency, adaptive testing can markedly increase the reliability of scores. As a result, comparisons across the cohorts of models using test scores could be biased by differences in reliability. Adjustments for differences in reliability were made more difficult by the methods used to scale the two tests and the analytical models used in this report.

Estimating Overall Reliability

The HSB and NELS tests were scaled using three-parameter logistic IRT models. In IRT models, in contrast to some traditional scaling models, no overall estimate of reliability is estimated. Instead, the definition of reliability is conditional on student proficiency.

In some traditional models, reliability is often assumed to be constant across levels of performance. In this case, the standard error of measurement (SEM) is a simple function of the reliability, $r_{xx'}$

$$SEM = [\sigma_x^2(1 - r_{xx'})]^{1/2} \tag{E.1}$$

That is, the SEM is simply the root of the error variance.

In contrast, in IRT models, the analog of the SEM, called the standard error of estimation (SE), is assumed to be conditional on an individual's level of performance. The SE is defined as

$$SE(\hat{\theta}) = \frac{1}{\sqrt{I(\theta)}} \tag{E.2}$$

where θ is the IRT estimate of proficiency and I, the test information function, is the sum of the item information functions at a given level of θ.

For any given θ, the reliability of the estimate can therefore be obtained by solving Eq. E.1 for $r_{xx'}$ and substituting in the IRT definition of the SE from Eq. E.2:

$$r_{\hat{\theta}\hat{\theta}'} = 1 - \frac{1}{[I(\theta)]\sigma_{\hat{\theta}}^2} \qquad (E.3)$$

An approximation of the overall reliability of the test can therefore be obtained by taking a weighted average of the information values in Eq. E.3, where the weights are the design weights used in the analysis:

$$\bar{r}_{\hat{\theta}\hat{\theta}'} = 1 - \frac{1}{\sigma_{\hat{\theta}}^2 \dfrac{\sum w[I(\theta)]}{\sum w}} \qquad (E.4)$$

Because BILOG provides a graphical display of test information as a function of θ but no machine-readable numerical estimates, this reliability coefficient was estimated using the information values from graphical output in intervals of 0.25 θ and calculating weighted averages of those values. This procedure yields for our samples estimated reliabilities of 0.917 for HSB and 0.954 for NELS, both high but discrepant enough to leave the possibility of bias in comparisons across the two cohorts.

Accounting for Reliability Differences in Analysis

Ways to account for measurement error in the dependent variable in multilevel models are poorly developed. To obtain a rough estimate of the severity of this problem in our models, we specified OLS models with individual and aggregate variables used in some of our multilevel models and estimated them with and without correction for measurement error. This indicated that some adjustments for measurement error were warranted.

The most complete OLS model used in this analysis was a contextual model that included 14 student-level variables, the school aggregates of these variables, and two macro variables (variables that do not vary within level 1 units). The student-level variables were dummies for African American, Hispanic, and female; four dummies for income groups; a dummy for college-prep track; math θ; mother's education; and four dummies indicating the highest level of mathematics course taken. The two macro-level variables were dummies for rural and urban school location.

Table E.1 presents the differences in parameter estimates from NELS and HSB (HSB subtracted from NELS), with and without correction for measurement error, and the arithmetic and percentage differences caused by the correction.

Variables are sorted in descending order of the absolute value of the percentage differences. Twelve of the 30 variables had percentage differences in excess of 75, and seven showed percentage differences of 170 or greater. However, most of these variables had very small parameter estimates, and the large percentage differences therefore corresponded to very small and unimportant arithmetic differences in estimates. A few variables, however, showed both large enough parameter estimates and sufficient effect of reliability that their interpretation

Table E.1

**Differences Between NELS and HSB: Estimates from Contextual Models
With and Without Correction for Measurement Error**

Variable	Uncorrected	Corrected	Arithmetic Difference	Percentage Difference
African American	–0.001	–0.009	–0.008	598.5
Income group 2	–0.001	0.003	0.004	–571.0
Proportion algebra 1	0.003	0.020	0.016	509.6
S mean proportion Hispanic	0.012	–0.036	–0.048	–385.4
S proportion income group 5	–0.009	–0.036	–0.027	318.7
S proportion income group 1	0.005	0.013	0.009	175.6
S mean math θ	0.015	–0.011	–0.026	–170.4
S proportion college prep	–0.040	–0.005	0.035	–87.1
S proportion female	0.016	0.002	–0.013	–86.2
S mean proportion advanced	–0.025	–0.004	0.022	–85.5
Hispanic	–0.019	–0.035	–0.016	85.0
S proportion African American	0.071	0.015	–0.056	–78.4
Income group 1	–0.020	–0.027	–0.007	35.8
Intercept	–0.136	–0.176	–0.040	29.1
Proportion geometry	–0.118	–0.094	0.024	–20.0
College prep	0.072	0.085	0.013	18.5
Proportion advanced	–0.168	–0.142	0.027	–15.8
S proportion income group 2	–0.093	–0.079	0.014	–15.3
Math θ	0.131	0.111	–0.020	–15.0
Proportion algebra 2	–0.181	–0.155	0.025	–14.1
S mean proportion algebra 2	–0.021	–0.019	0.003	–13.1
S rural	–0.023	–0.027	–0.003	13.1
Income group 4	–0.010	–0.009	0.001	–12.4
S mean mother's education	0.068	0.075	0.007	10.6
Female	–0.085	–0.092	–0.007	8.0
Mother's education	0.016	0.017	0.001	4.8
S urban	0.065	0.062	–0.003	–4.8
Income group 5	0.043	0.041	–0.002	–4.5
S mean proportion geometry	–0.167	–0.162	0.005	–2.8
S proportion income group 4	–0.102	–0.104	–0.002	2.0
S mean proportion algebra 1	–0.250	–0.251	–0.001	0.5

NOTE: Initial S denotes a school-level variable.

would be altered by correcting for unreliability. An example is the school proportion African American.

Most important for our purposes is the effect of reliability differences on the parameter estimates for student-level mathematics θ. This effect was modest. However, because of the importance of this estimate for this report, the estimates of the correlations between grades and θ (in the analysis of changing-correlation inflation) were corrected for unreliability. Because the interpretation of other coefficients is less important and the methods for correcting multilevel models are poorly developed, we did not correct the multilevel models for unreliability. Therefore, only sizable differences in the parameter estimates between HSB and NELS should be accepted with confidence.

Bibliography

Adelman, C., "Devaluation, Diffusion and the College Connection: A Study of High School Transcripts, 1964–1981," paper presented at the Meeting of the National Commission on Excellence in Education, Washington, D.C., 1982.

Alexander, S., "Trophy Transcript Hunters Are Finding Professors Have Become an Easy Mark," *Wall Street Journal*, April 27, 1993, p. B1.

Berends, M., and D. Koretz, "Reporting Minority Students' Test Scores: How Well Can the National Assessment of Educational Progress Account for Differences in Social Context?" *Educational Assessment*, Vol. 3, No. 3, 1996, pp. 249–285.

Berends, M., T. Sullivan, and S. R. Lucas, "Examining Racial-Ethnic Test Score Differences in National Data: Equating Scores Among Several High School Senior Cohorts, 1972–1992," unpublished manuscript, RAND, 1999.

Birnbaum, R., "Factors Related to University Grade Inflation," *Journal of Higher Education*, Vol. 48, 1977, pp. 519–539.

Brookhart, S. M., "Teachers' Grading Practices: Meaning and Values," *Journal of Educational Measurement*, Vol. 30, No. 2, 1993, pp. 123–142.

Campbell, J. R., C. M. Hombo, and J. Mazzeo, *NAEP 1999 Trends in Academic Progress: Three Decades of Student Performance*, National Center for Educational Statistics, Office of Educational Research and Improvement, U.S. Department of Education, Washington, D.C., 2000.

de Gruijter, D.N.M., "A Comment on Some Standard Errors in Item Response Theory," *Psychometrka*, Vol. 49, No. 2, 1984, pp. 269–272.

Gamoran, A., "Measuring Curriculum Differentiation," *American Journal of Education*, Vol. 97, 1989, pp. 129–143.

Gamoran, A., and M. Berends, "Stratification in Secondary Schools," *Review of Educational Research*, Vol. 57, 1987, pp. 415–435.

Hambleton, R. K., "Principles and Selected Applications of Item Response Theory," in R. L. Linn (ed.), *Educational Measurement, Third Edition*, American Council on Education-Macmillan, New York, 1989, pp. 147–200.

Ingels, Steven J., Kathryn L. Dowd, John D. Baldridge, James L. Stipe, Virginia H. Bartot, and Martin R. Frankel, *NELS:88 Second Follow-Up: Student Component Data File User's Manual*, National Center for Education Statistics, Washington, D.C., 1993.

Ingels, Steven J., Kathryn L. Dowd, John R. Taylor, Virginia H. Bartot, Martin R. Frankel, and Paul A. Pulliam, *NELS:88 Second Follow-Up: Transcript Component*

Data File User's Manual, National Center for Education Statistics, Washington, D.C., 1995.

Jones, Calvin, Miriam Clark, Geraldine Mooney, Harold McWilliams, Ioanna Crawford, Bruce Stephenson, and Roger Tourangeau, *High School and Beyond 1980 Sophomore Cohort First Follow-Up 1982 Data File User's Manual,* National Center for Education Statistics, Washington, D.C., 1983a.

Jones, Calvin, Shirley Knight, Marjorie Butz, Ioanna Crawford, and Bruce Stephenson, *High School and Beyond Transcripts Survey (1982): Data File User's Manual,* National Center for Education Statistics, Washington, D.C., 1983b.

Keith, T. Z., "Time Spent on Homework and High School Grades: A Large-Sample Path Analysis," *Journal of Educational Psychology,* Vol. 74, No. 2, 1982, pp. 248–253.

Kolevzon, M. S. "Grade Inflation in Higher Education: A Comparative Study," *Research in Higher Education,* Vol. 15, No. 3, 1981, pp. 195-211.

Koretz, D., "What Happened to Test Scores, and Why?" *Educational Measurement: Issues and Practice,* Vol. 11, No. 4, Winter 1992, pp. 7–11.

Kreft, I., and J. DeLeeuw, *Introducing Multilevel Modeling,* Sage, London, 1998.

Levine, A. "To Deflated Grade Inflation, Simplify the System," *Chronicle of Higher Education,* January 14, 1994, p. B3.

Lord, F. M., *Evaluation with Artificial Data of a Procedure for Estimating Ability and Item Characteristic Curve Parameters,* Educational Testing Service, Research Bulletin 75-33, Princeton, New Jersey, 1975.

Lord, F. M., *Applications of Item Response to Theory to Practical Testing Problems,* Lawrence Erlbaum, Mahwah, New Jersey, 1980.

Lucas, S. R. *Tracking Inequality: Stratification and Mobility in American High Schools,* Teachers College Press, New York, 1999.

Murphy, J., *Restructuring Schools: Capturing and Assessing the Phenomena,* Teachers College Press, New York, 1991.

National Center for Education Statistics, *1998 Revision of the Secondary School Taxonomy,* U.S. Department of Education, Washington, D.C., 1999.

National Commission on Excellence in Education, *A Nation at Risk: The Imperative for Educational Reform,* U.S. Government Printing Office, Washington, D.C., 1983.

Pilcher, J. K., "The Value-Driven Meaning of Grades," *Educational Assessment,* Vol. 2, No. 1, 1994, pp. 69–88.

Rock, D. A., and J. M. Pollack, *Psychometric Report for the NELS:88 Base Year Through Second Follow-Up,* National Center for Education Statistics, Washington, D.C., 1995.

Rock, D. A., R. B. Ekstrom, M. E. Goertz, T. L. Hilton, and J. M. Pollack, *Factors Associated with Decline of Test Scores of High School Seniors, 1972 to 1980.* Educational Testing Service, NCES 85-218, Princeton, New Jersey, 1985a

Rock, D. A., T. L. Hilton, J. M. Pollack, R. B. Ekstrom, and M. E. Goertz, *Psychometric Analysis of the NLS and the High School and Beyond Test Batteries,* National Center for Education Statistics, Washington, D.C., 1985b.

Rogers, G. G., A Time Series Approach to the Longitudinal Study of Undergraduate Grades, University of Northern Iowa, Department of Educational Psychology, ERIC Document Reproduction Service no. ED 235 228, Cedar Falls, Iowa, 1983.

Soloman, W., "Class Rank a Problem for Student with Straight A's," *Allentown Morning Call*, May 10, 1998a, pp. A1, A4.

Soloman, W., "Parkland Graduation Makes Perfect Sense," *Allentown Morning Call*, June 9, 1998b, pp. B5.

Stiggins, R. J., D. A. Frisbie, and P. Griswold, "Inside High School Grading Practices: Building a Research Agenda," *Educational Measurement: Issues and Practice,* Vol. 8, No. 2, 1989, pp. 5–14.

Stone, J. E., "Inflated Grades, Inflated Enrollment, and Inflated Budgets: An Analysis and Call for Review at the State Level,"*Educational Policy Analysis Archives*, Vol. 3, No. 11, 1995, pp. 1–31, available at http://www.epaa.asu. edu/epaa/v3n11.htm.

Swaminathan, H., and J. A. Gifford, "Bayesian Estimation in the Three-Parameter Logistic Model," *Psychometrika*, Vol. 51, No. 4, 1986, pp. 589–601.

Thissen, D. M., and H. Wainer, *Some Supporting Evidence for Lord's Guideline for Estimating "c,"* Educational Testing Service, Research Bulletin No. 85-57, Princeton, New Jersey, 1985.

Turnbull, W. W., *Student Change, Program Change: Why SAT Scores Kept Falling,* College Entrance Examination Board, College Board Rep. No. 85-2, New York, 1985.

U.S. Department of Education, *What Do Student Grades Mean? Differences Across Schools,* Research Report, January 1994.

Ziomek, R. L., and J. C. Svec, *High School Grades and Achievement: Evidence of Grade Inflation,* American College Testing Program, ACT Research Report Series 95-3, Iowa City, Iowa, 1995.

Zirkel, P. A., "Grade Inflation: A Leadership Opportunity for Schools of Education?" *Teachers College Record*, Vol. 101, No. 2, 1999, pp. 247–260.